More Praise for Fresh Expressions
of People Over Property

"The purpose of Fresh Expressions is the formation of new Christian communities—being church with people who don't go to church. It can be easy to falsely assume that our church buildings are an obstacle to this work. However, as Carter and Warren show, a building, missionally repurposed for the sake of the greater community can be one of the greatest assets we have to reach new people."

–Michael Beck, Director of Re-Missioning for Fresh Expressions U.S., Cultivator of Fresh Expressions for the Florida Conference UMC, and Director/Adjunct Professor Fresh Expressions House of Studies at United Theological Seminary; author, *A Field Guide to Methodist Fresh Expressions; Deep Roots, Wild Branches*, and *Contextual Intelligence: Unlocking the Ancient Secret to Front Line Mission*, from Abingdon Press

"I'm excited—this new practical resource hits square in the "strike zone" for what so many churches are seeking today, as they grapple with the potential of imaginatively leveraging the missional usefulness of their property for the next season. I can hardly wait to recommend *Fresh Expressions of People Over Property* as an additional, crucial handhold of renewal for congregations everywhere."

–Rev. Sue Nilson Kibbey, author, *Floodgates: Holy Momentum for a Fearless Church*, from Abingdon Press

"Imbuing property with a missional focus helps churches reach people with the grace of Jesus Christ who we might otherwise never engage. That is the message of this book that I heartily endorse. Audrey Warren and Ken Carter offer compelling stories of Christian leaders rethinking sacred space and mobile mission with great imagination and creativity. Read it with an open heart and we may see opportunities for mission that we've never considered before."

–Robert Schnase, United Methodist Bishop and author of *Five Practices of Fruitful Congregations Revised and Updated*, from Abingdon Press

"By putting people over property, churches can regain their focus on what's truly important in terms of outreach and missions. Warren and Carter challenge church leaders to look beyond their structures and enter into an unknown future with steps of faith to tell the gospel story in new ways and in new places."

–Rosairo "Roz" Picardo, Dean of The Chapel, Director of the Pohly Leadership Center, co-pastor of Mosaic Church at United Theological Seminary

"The next step in driving the Fresh Expressions movement forward is creative thinking about how our church property can reach people for Jesus in new ways. This book reminds us who the church is: the church is the people, not the building. If you find yourself in a community that, through desire or necessity, needs to think in new ways about reaching your neighbors, this work gives you the tools to go about that mission."

–Michelle J. Morris, pastor and author of *Gospel Discipleship: Four Pathways for Christian Disciples*, from Abingdon Press

"Carter and Warren offer a wonderful antidote to the 'Christian imagination deficit disorder' that is afflicting the American mainline church. Through stories, practical projects, and thoughtful analysis, Carter and Warren offer signs of hope for faithful witness in the turbulent times in which we live. Be inspired, and put experiments into action wherever you are!"

–L. Gregory Jones, Dean of Duke Divinity School, Durham, NC

AUDREY WARREN
KENNETH H. CARTER JR.

FRESH EXPRESSIONS of
PEOPLE
OVER
PROPERTY

Scripture, Stories, and Strategies to Help
People of Faith Reimagine Their Space

Abingdon Press™
Nashville

LCCN: 2020941324
ISBN: 978-1-7910-0475-0

Scripture quotations unless noted otherwise are from the Common English Bible. Copyright © 2011 by the Common English Bible. All rights reserved. Used by permission. www.CommonEnglishBible.com.

From page 54, "Won't You Be My Neighbor?" written by Fred Rogers, © 1967, Fred M. Rogers. Used with permission.

20 21 22 23 24 25 26 27 28 29—10 9 8 7 6 5 4 3 2 1
MANUFACTURED IN THE UNITED STATES OF AMERICA

CONTENTS

**Other Abingdon Press Books by
Audrey Warren and Kenneth H. Carter Jr.**

*Fresh Expressions: A New Kind of Methodist
Church for People Not in Church*

**Other Fresh Expressions books from
Abingdon Press**

A Field Guide to Methodist Fresh Expressions
by Michael Beck with Jorge Acevedo

ACKNOWLEDGMENTS

Deepest gratitude for Branches United Methodist Church and First United Methodist Church of Miami for trusting God more than all else and teaching me and the world what a courageous faith is all about! Sincere thanks to the people who shared their stories in this book. Your lives and work have been soup for my soul and hope for my heart! Thankful for my colleagues in ministry in the Florida Conference who are serving local churches and outreach ministries. We are in this work together and each of you teach me and love me and inspire me every darn day! May we continue to learn, be courageous, fail and get up again, and do the hard-work and the heart-work that we have been so privileged to be called to by God. Most of all I am humbled once again to work with Bishop Ken Carter who has been a mentor and a friend. This book is deeper theologically because of Bishop Carter. The spiritual leadership he provides for all of his work is admirable and shows up here many times!

–Audrey Warren

In gratitude to Audrey Warren—for her conceptual vision for this book, and more deeply for her reflective engagement with sacred spaces and risk-taking leadership in helping us to reimagine them. And for all who love the local church, and more deeply the purpose of the local church, to bear witness to the love of God in real communities, among those who hunger for mercy, justice and reconciliation.

–Kenneth H. Carter Jr.

INTRODUCTION

Our first book together, *Fresh Expressions: A New Kind of Methodist Church for People Not in Church*, circulated widely as part of an innovation movement that began in England and is spreading in the United States. One might ask why this book about church assets can carry the name of a movement created for people not in the church, both spiritually and physically. Transformed buildings are not inherently Fresh Expressions. However, for many congregations, the bricks or siding of their buildings are leverage and collateral for the birth of Fresh Expressions. Property is a sign of how people are invested in a community.

It's common knowledge that, for more than fifty years, established denominations in the United States have not grown but have continued to decline in participation and revenue. Even if they could, Fresh Expressions of ministry are not meant to replace the "traditioned" churches that share theological and social identities with other churches. Rather, the aim is to create space for new people, in new places, and in new ways to experience a life-changing relationship with Jesus Christ. The "traditioned" church and Fresh Expressions form an ecosystem that feeds each other. During decline, church leaders typically experience the stress of unpaid bills, broken toilets, and leaking roofs. Budgets are cut to a minimum, funding a full-time pastor at best and maintaining a building with a questionable lifespan.

The word *decline* is not often associated with risk, yet in the pan-Methodist family, we've seen congregations around the world take great risk despite decline. Most of those risks involve leveraging property to reach more people. In most cases, Fresh Expressions are birthed in the process *and* the "traditioned" church benefits from renewed energy, life, and mission. Fresh Expressions are particularly suited to declining congregations because they are neither the next shiny new thing nor a grand idea. The stories documented in this book show how the transformation of property with a focus on mission (and not only maintenance) can give birth to new forms of church.

The phrase "People over Property" can evoke discomfort in some congregations. Some might characterize the idea as "simplistic," since many established faith communities are committed to the idea that a church needs property. When we say that people are more important than property, we encounter tough questions that all faith communities are asking these days about their assets and resources. Rather than advise congregations to sell their property to get top dollar, we invite readers and churches into a conversation through *story, scripture,* and *strategy.* This approach helps each faith community understand and potentially transform their sacred spaces. In his role as bishop, Ken has walked alongside some churches and leaders who did creative work in reimagining their future. In other churches, leaders avoided thinking beyond their own experiences and preferences. We confess that this struggle—to hunker down or reboot—lies within each of our hearts and minds.

Many who grew up in a church were taught the lyrics to "We Are the Church" early in their faith journey. The song's basic theme is "the church is not a building, the church is a people."[1] Audrey remembers acting out the dance motions to each line with second-grade friends

---

1. Richard K. Avery and Donald S. Marsh, "We Are the Church" (Carol Stream, IL: Hope Publishing Co., 1972).

and then, at the command of the children's director, shouting the last line of the first verse, "The church is a people." Although this song may be engraved in childhood faith memories, as we mature and obtain property, the message typically does not sustain the power that was conveyed through the shouts of second graders.

Many churches around the country continue to sing this song, but their financial statements sing a different one. Our budgets reflect a priority of property over people. During a four-year period, I (Audrey) worked with twenty-three churches with budget data that document spending more money maintaining a building than providing for their people in mission, programing, and staffing. Jim Wallis, founder of *Sojourners*, observes that our church budgets are moral documents.[2] Our budgets tell us what we care about and who we are. Our personal budgets do the same. With regret, I downloaded the financial budgeting app, Mint, that taught me things that I believed were not true.

Prior to downloading the app, I described myself as someone who did not eat fast food except when traveling. Yet within one week I exceeded my fast food budget for the month, though I did not travel more than ten miles that week. I believed one thing about myself, but I learned it was not true when the data was placed in front of me. The truth: I *loved* the Doritos Locos Tacos Supreme from Taco Bell. In fact, kale was not part of my weekly diet at the time, and Taco Bell tacos were there at least once a week. I had to face the music—I was a fast-food eater.

In the same way, as pastors and participants we think we are living out the values and moral choices we were taught and believe. However, when data is before us, we are confronted with a revealing story that has become our reality. We notice habits that took priority to simply survive and keep going. We discover that we, in fact, care

2. Jim Wallis, *Rediscovering Values: A Guide for Economic and Moral Recovery* (Brentwood, TN: Howard Books, 2011).

more about our property than our people. Our budgets are laden with patchwork maintenance requests, and our fundraising campaigns are for a new air conditioner instead of youth mission trips for the summer. Unfortunately, even though most of our budgets are spent on our buildings, many churches have become (in the words of a friend) "the church of the grey cross and the pink flame."

So what choice do our churches have? Do we simply spiral down and depreciate until we cannot pay the bills anymore? Do we sell all of our sacred spaces and move into store fronts, streets, and homes? If the church is the people, then why do we need buildings? Are our temples simply tombstones to traditions of the past? In honest moments with God these questions keep me up at night. When I shouted, "The church is a people," I did not know the power this song would have for me and the two churches I have served so far.

The first church building came down not through introspection, prayer, discernment, and a hundred meetings. Rather during my first Pentecost season as a pastor, it came down in the middle of the night due to a fire that started on the playground. The sanctuary, which was at one time the education hall, and the playground were condemned. As we gathered in the midst of smoke and ashes, we proclaimed the same words loud and proud, "The church is a people." We affirmed this, and it gave us hope as we mourned that day. But what were we mourning? If the church is a people, what meaning comes from the building for our life together in a faith and community?

The day after the fire, a young man came to the scene, where he sat and cried. He told me later that he grew up in the church and in the afterschool program, Branches. The young man drove five hours south when he heard the news. He was tired since he and his wife had just returned from Israel. He reflected on his trip to the Holy Land and, while weeping on the ruins of the church, he shared that the Branches building felt more holy than any of the sites he visited in Israel. The old one-room church was where he first met God, and it changed his life. So, space can be sacred. Perhaps we should not sell all of our churches? Perhaps our sanctuaries should not be turned into basketball courts and bingo halls? Can we avoid doing so?

Let's dive into some complex questions about sacred space and mobile mission. Together we'll explore scripture, stories, and strategies that help churches be faithful to their people and the property they have been given. Through the narratives of scripture, we read that God's people often celebrated the promise and gift of land. The book of Exodus details exactly how the meeting tent (or tabernacle) should be built. Certainly, there is a purpose for sacred space in biblical times and in our world today. Through our experiences with coworkers in ministry, we have gleaned some of the successes and failures to assist churches in this precarious time. We hope and pray that this book will be a practical guide for church leaders who work together to ask hard questions, to be creative, and to move into the faithful practice of placing people over property.

Chapter 1

#TentLife[1]

And the word became flesh and pitched his tent among us.

–John 1:14[2]

How does a congregation embrace a #tentlife? The very first worship space dedicated by our faith ancestors was located in a meeting tent. In the books of Exodus and Numbers the tent moved! Their journey to the promised land was not paved on roads but required flexibility, great faith, and courage.

Once again, God's people find themselves navigating drastic change. In the twenty-first century, 39 percent of churches in the United States are growing and 38 percent of churches are declining.[3] But, far and wide, the church is experiencing a cycle of fear, uncertainty, and doubt. In *The Great Emergence*, the late Phyllis Tickle observed that every five hundred years the church gets turned upside down and emerges again in a "Fresh Way."[4] Tickle claims that we are currently experiencing a five-hundred-year revolution.

However, when we look closely at individual congregations, it does not appear that most are being turned upside down or

---

1. Chapter titles are rendered in the form of Twitter hashtags.
2. Author translation; compare "The word became flesh and made his home among us" (CEB).
3. "National Study of Congregations' Economic Practices," Lake Institute on Faith and Giving, 2020, https://www.nscep.org/lake-institute/.
4. Phyllis Tickle, *The Great Emergence: How Christianity Is Changing and Why* (Grand Rapids, MI: Baker Reprint, 2012).

embracing something fresh. We see churches in decline, closing, and falling into disrepair. Many churches are opting to slowly slip into "sleep mode" until their power runs out and they eventually shut down. The glimpses of transformation, growth, and freshness are present, and they are most of the time found in churches and leaders who are willing to take risks. The risks often look like getting back to basics, "pruning the trees," and pitching some tents.

In this chapter we share stories, scripture, and strategies that help congregations to understand and embrace a #tentlife. As the Israelites learned, the tent life was not the plan, but rather where God's people found themselves as faithful and free people. *The movement toward tent life typically does not occur out of a detailed five-year project plan but is often initiated during times of desperation.* The first story below recounts what happened in a church transformed through destruction and desperation. The second story takes place at a church in Northern Ireland, where, through reconciliation, a small mission became a beacon of hope and healing for thousands. This church was motivated out of a deep desire to declare a new word of hope in the aftermath of war.

Story 1—Branches United Methodist Church, Florida City, FL

A fire on Pentecost is ironic, but not unusual. Many of us can picture children with construction paper flames attached to their foreheads by a stapled construction paper headband. Pentecost at my first church as a pastor was too literal. At 1:00 a.m., I received a call and heard words that have become common in our struggling and aging church buildings: "the church is on fire." I immediately jumped out of bed and drove down to the church to find our sweet sanctuary in flames.

The sanctuary was actually the education building. The previously named Florida City United Methodist Church vowed to rebuild their sanctuary after Hurricane Betsy destroyed it, but with limited funds the church could only afford an education hall and believed that could serve the purposes of worship and fellowship until they rebuilt. The dream to rebuild a sanctuary was never realized. However, other purposes were later realized for the small congregation that found itself rooted in the middle of an immigrant community by the 1970s.

The early 1990s brought more change for the church and community when Hurricane Andrew destroyed most homes and buildings in the area. Florida City is just south of Homestead, Florida, where Hurricane Andrew hit land. A widely circulated photo showed a row of intact Habitat for Humanity homes surrounded by completely devastated houses. The nightmare of Hurricane Andrew led to new dreams for the small United Methodist church. The church education building became the headquarters for the United Methodist Committee on Relief (UMCOR) for a few years after Hurricane Andrew. Missionaries from around the state and country also came to the small town.

Kim King Torres, a missionary through the Church and Community Worker program of the General Board of Global Ministries of the UMC, stayed. She started an afterschool program at the church that would become known as "Branches." Because Hurricane Andrew blew out the windows of the small church, Kim was able to help the church find its neighbors again. Although difficult at times, the relationship between the church and afterschool program strengthened them both and helped them be part of God's mission in Florida City.

Through Kim and her husband, Ray, and many other volunteers and staff, the church and afterschool program evolved into a center for mission and outreach to the community. *Morning, noon, and night the property had a purpose.* By morning a food pantry and legal clinic, by day an afterschool program, and by night a center for English classes and Bible studies. In many ways the needs of the people determined what happened on the property. One would think this changed on May 23, 2010, Pentecost Sunday, when we received the news that the church was on fire, but it did not.

On May 24, 2010, a very large tent was erected outside the other small house on the property. That day we began our #tentlife. For the next eight months we worshipped under the tent, English in the morning and Spanish in the evening. During the week we tutored under the tent, ate meals under the tent, and even had office space under the tent. #Tentlife became a phrase used among our volunteers, staff, and church members when we would put into action a clever or ridiculous idea to improve our tent. For example, our tent arrived during rainy season, so the Florida dirt quickly became mud. #Tentlife required us to cover the floor with cardboard one Sunday. This went on until we finally covered the ground with rocks donated by a friend in construction. The rain not only affected the floor but at times during worship or tutoring rain would start striking down in a diagonal direction, soaking those sitting by the sides. In that instance, #tentlife required that we make roll-up sides out of blue tarps for our tent.

The #tentlife did not last forever. After the tent, we moved into an eight-foot-wide trailer, then, after two years, to the elementary school for a summer. After this we moved to City Hall, until we finally moved into our new building in October 2014. In many ways we felt like the Israelites circling Florida City until we reached the promised land. The new building quickly became a target, and we had two burglaries in our first six months. Yet our time in the #tentlife proved to be valuable because it taught us flexibility, courage, and persistence. Together, over four long years, we embraced the life of a missionary and grew. Out of destruction and desperation, old property was redeveloped and created for several purposes that served the mission of the church and community.

Desperation is not the only factor that might encourage a #tentlife. Declaration is often the motivation for a church moving into a missionary space. In the apartheid era in South Africa, Central Methodist Mission opened a coffee shop for *all* people—white, black, and brown—to eat together. The shop was an outreach and a holy space. They set up a tent, a space without walls, doors, gates, or locks in the community. They did this to declare the gospel message of inclusivity. More recently, a small mission in Northern Ireland was inspired to declare a message of reconciliation.

Story 2—East Belfast Mission and Skainos

During the civil, sectarian war in Northern Ireland, there were spaces and churches where Catholics were excluded and others where Protestants were excluded. Many books have been written about this time in Northern Ireland's history, known as "the Troubles." The motivations, reasons, and purposes of the Troubles are complex and confusing, even to those who lived through it. Whatever the goals were by either party, one goal was achieved—a drastic turn away from organized religion. Churches saw major decline during the Troubles and in the decades following. Religion was enveloped by politics to the point that political perspectives were absolutely associated with either Catholic or Protestant factions. Arguments were not about the trinity or virgin birth but rather focused on Northern Ireland's relationship with Great Britain.

Younger generations had little tolerance for political riffs posing as religious rigor. The lasting consequence of the Troubles for the church has been a loss of respect and trust. Churches and pastors could have a variety of responses to this reality. One response could be "it wasn't me," citing that the Troubles were long ago when pastors and leaders were simply children and had no say in the matter. Another response could be one of justification for the church's behavior through the Troubles and one of anger toward the reality and reaction of the culture and the church further separating itself from people on the streets. A third reaction could be to simply slowly die and do nothing.

Through the courageous leadership of Gary Mason, the East Belfast Mission chose a fourth way: the way of deep listening, transformation, and declaration. East Belfast Mission is located in the depth of an impoverished Unionist Protestant community. When Gary arrived, the small mission church was struggling with about one hundred fifty people in worship each week. Within the first year they lost fifty to sixty of those people due to death alone. While the members aged, so did the building. Housed in the church building were church missions with the homeless and less fortunate. Prior to arriving at the church, Gary spent much of his ministry in the work of reconciliation and peace for his beloved country. Two of the pro Protestant militia groups read their decommissioning of weapons statement at Gary's church. Gary, a Unionist Protestant, made it his ministry to bring people together and proclaim the gospel message of equality and love. Gary brought this agenda to the East Belfast Mission, and soon the small group of dedicated disciples shared in the vision.

The transformation they hoped for was birthed out of a desire to make a declaration that God loves all people, and all are welcome to God's great tent. The small Protestant church began hosting courses in the Irish language, which was highly controversial but made the declaration that the church was about the work of reconciliation and unity, and not about separation. The mission grew through their ministry with addiction programs, such as Alcoholics Anonymous.

Gradually the mission knew it would need a new building to host the many groups that were meeting each day. Their vision was to build on a city block next to their mission. The new space would include a sanctuary, chapel, affordable housing, community space, a community café and restaurant, and a resale store. The budget for the project was 21 million pounds. The small group of disciples did not have these funds, but those who believed in their mission did. In just a few years the money was raised through government grants and outside funding sources.

They named their new building Skainos, which means "the tent" in Greek. The purpose of the building is to include all people in God's great mission and promise. The idea of the tent also came from the story of the Israelites in the Old Testament. When I spoke with Gary, he described four main reasons for the name Skainos. First, the connection with tents in the Old Testament. God's presence was known in a tent, so to live in a tent is to live with God and commit to a permanent pilgrimage. Second, the way in which a tent describes the movement of God through Jesus into the world as seen in alternative translations of John 1:14,[5] "the word became flesh and pitched his tent among us." Third, the meaning and use of tent in 2 Corinthians 5:1-4 where Paul reminds his readers that the physical "tents" of this world such as our bodies and buildings are perishable, and nothing compared to the eternal home God is preparing for us. This verse is special to their church, because it reminds them that although they built something glorious and even missional, it is not the final goal of their faith and mission. Fourth, a tent is an image of a structure that encourages looking outside. This image is important for the personal and communal spiritual growth of the church.

Through the faith and risk-taking of church members and their leader, Gary, the missional church was able to actualize their goal and

---

5. Author translation; compare "The word became flesh and made his home among us" (CEB).

expand their ministries far beyond what they could ask or imagine. The worshipping community continues to meet on Sunday under new pastoral leadership. The "Tent" or Skainos includes community gardens, affordable housing, a community café, rental space for community groups, Irish language courses, resale store, Alcoholics Anonymous, and many other ministries and mission groups that work toward building the gospel message of peace and reconciliation in Belfast. The leadership of Skainos continues to look outside of itself and build relationships with its neighbors, its city, and its country.

Both stories in this chapter feature churches who were inspired by the story of the Israelites under a tent in the desert. Whether their #tentlife came about due to desperation or declaration, both have embraced a new way of life that produces fruit in their life as a church and in their community.

Scripture

For centuries, faith communities have related their story to the Israelites in the book of Exodus. Some can link their story as people freed from slavery, while others find themselves in a wilderness. In either case, dislocation and the search for freedom occurs due to circumstances out of their control. As our cultures continue to change and diversify, and as our churches emerge under duress, biblical stories about land, people, ancestors, and property can guide us.

Land as Promise and Problem

In *The Land*, Walter Brueggemann observes that "land is a central . . . theme of biblical faith."[6] A typical Bible reader can easily identify this theme when reading the stories. The Old Testament

---

6. Walter Brueggemann, *The Land* (Philadelphia: Fortress Press, 1977), 3.

hinges on stories about the exodus and the exile, as God's people seek security in a promised land, whether building a house for God or mourning its destruction. While Jesus is described in the New Testament as one who has "no place to lay his head,"[7] the Pauline Letters are all written to churches in specific cities and places. Furthermore, the New Testament is looking toward a new promised land, as in the New Heaven and the New Earth.

The importance of land as a biblical motif is not simply possession of property. In scripture we see that land and property and afterlife are directly connected to faith. Whether God's people are in plenty or want in relation to land, the way they move through property is often a reflection of their faith, or lack thereof. Walter Brueggemann also describes land as a point of promise *and* a problem. The waves of promise and problem flow through the Old Testament. Beginning with Abraham one can see a movement from "landlessness" to "landedness."[8] God calls Abraham to landlessness. This calling is freely chosen and is accepted as an act of faith.[9] Landlessness is accepted because there is a promise of land and children, as many as the stars in the sky. The promise is fulfilled until starvation drives Abraham's progeny from the land in Egypt.

In the book of Exodus, God's people multiply without land while slaves in Egypt until they leave to seek the promised land once again. The first chapter of Exodus tells of the great jealousy and fear the Egyptians had for the Israelites in their midst. The promise of freedom accompanied the necessity to exist for a while as landless people. With great faith, the Israelites followed Moses into the desert as wanderers. Brueggemann differentiates between wanderers and sojourners. Sojourners know the direction they are going, whereas the

---

7. Luke 9:58.
8. Brueggeman, *The Land*, 6.
9. Brueggeman, *The Land*, 7.

wanderer is "not on the way anywhere."[10] After many battles such as the one in Jericho, Israel finally finds itself settled.

The landedness described in 1 and 2 Samuel show once again that the "land that promised to create space for human joy and freedom became the very source of dehumanizing exploitation and oppression."[11] Land and possessions that held great promise quickly turned into a problem. Not long after a time of landedness, Israel experiences the exile, which is the subject of many psalms. Israel vacillates back to landlessness. In the words of the Psalms, one can point to deep pain, which is often reprised by remembering the promise made to ancestors. These moments of landlessness trigger lament but also memory that hope persists despite the circumstances. Brueggemann writes, "Precisely in the context of landlessness do the promises loom large. It is in the emptiness of Israel, exposed and without resources, that promises are received with power, that risks are run, and hope is energizing."[12]

The last movement back to the land involves the community of Ezra and Nehemiah. To stay landed the people of Israel decide not to rule over the land like powerful kings but rather in a spirit of purity and obedience. After many years they learned that their frugality did not lead to fruit in the land as expected, and like previous cycles, Israel once more had no choice but to let their land go to foreign forces more powerful than they were. Once again, the Israelites were landless; even frugality and pruning could not save their sacred space.

The Meeting Tent

Whether Israel was landed or without a "meeting tent" is a common problem throughout the Old Testament and into the New

10. Brueggeman, *The Land*, 8.
11. Brueggeman, *The Land*, 11.
12. Brueggeman, *The Land*, 9.

Testament (Acts 18) after the destruction of the second temple. During times of wandering, God directs Israel to erect a tent and make it their place of worship. In Exodus 25 we find the detailed instructions about exotic dyes and types of wood acceptable for the tent. The tent did not stay in one place, but moved by the presence of God, as imagined in the lightning or cloud that hovered over the tent. Numbers 33 describes for us the journey of the tent. In many ways, the journey is experienced today as a new church start looking for the right home!

The tent did not stay in one place, nor was a new one built in every location. The same tent was picked up, moved, and erected in each location in the desert. According to Numbers 33 the tent was moved roughly thirty times in the span of forty years, about every fifteen months. The word in Hebrew for this structure was *mishkan*, which means tent, abode, or dwelling place. The tent's purpose is revealed as the place where God dwelt among the Israelites while they wandered.

Israel's #tentlife, landlessness, and landedness is not simply a theological reflection about space, place, and sanctuary. God's presence in the covenant is bound inextricably through Israel's relationship to the land and to the meeting tent. These ties are instructive and normal as we too experience land, buildings, meeting tents, and sanctuaries as the source of our promises and problems. Could it be that the faith, flexibility, and perseverance are among the strategies the church should embrace as we work toward a faithful future in a changing culture?

In our book *Fresh Expressions: A New Kind of Methodist Church for People Not in Church*, we refer to the work of sociologist Ray Oldenburg in identifying "third places." The first two places are where we live (house, apartment) and where we work. In a church culture, the third place was the church building, where we spent many hours a week in worship, Sunday school, choir practice, committee meetings, and recreation. In a few settings this remains a reality, but it is steadily fading from the culture and especially among younger demographics.

New third places are emerging: pubs, coffee shops, sports leagues, book clubs, art galleries, digital experiences. As you enter into these third spaces, you might ask the question, How can areas with church buildings become third places for the community itself? This is a #tentlife concept too, and it will require a reimagining of space and a flexibility of resource usage.

Strategies

Faith—Honesty

Faith is a virtue, and faithfulness is a spiritual fruit, but it is also a strategy necessary for fruitfulness in ministry together. Faith may seem implied in the work of renewing Christian communities, yet our declining numbers and constant quarrels reveal that fear is in fact directing our behaviors in the church at large, and in many local churches. Fear keeps our heads in the sand about where we are and where we need to be going. It's time to embrace the #tentlife, to grab hold of God's newness that awaits us. With a good-faith effort, let's look at the realities of our life together. By and large, churches are spending more money on property than people. The majority of our largest givers are aging. Most of our buildings do not meet handicap accessibility codes and some are filled with mold that could pose health problems to our participants.

The time has come for us to speak about our land and property as both promise *and* problem. Our honesty might lead us to land-lessness. Or, for a few, it might lead to greater landedness, but either way we are seeking a way out of chaos into a place of knowledge and freedom.

Unfortunately, to simply survive many churches let their properties go into disrepair, such that the property controls the church. Random renters determine the hours the church can use certain spaces. The water explosion in the choir room drove the choir to move into the sanctuary, which changes how worship begins *and* means the choir cannot move back into the moldy choir room. Possibly you can relate, even laugh a little, or cry a little. When we look into these unfortunate circumstances, we know that we do not look alone. God's presence walks with us and fills us with hope as we follow in faith.

A Missionary Spirit

Paul was clearly the most influential missionary in the New Testament. It seems appropriate that Paul funded his missionary work first by physically making tents (Acts 18). Yes, Paul used his hands for his side hustle, which was making tents to sustain his mission of spreading the gospel. #Tentlife gave Paul flexibility to move across the Gentile world. Tent-making is a theme in stories old and new about freedom for God's people. More than simply a physical dwelling, the tent is an essential strategy to help the church reimagine its mission and sacred space.

When addressing clergy as bishop, I (Ken) build on the insight of Kennon Callahan: "The age of the professional pastor is over, and the age of the missional pastor has begun."[13] The missionary church is sustained by this #tentlife.

The Fresh Expressions movement, which began in England, brought renewal and growth to the Anglican Church and the British Methodist Church. Most of their leaders are missionaries or children of missionaries. A missionary spirit can mean many things. While we don't want to limit the meaning by too narrow a definition, from

---

13. Kennon L. Callahan, *Effective Church Leadership: Building on the Twelve Keys* (San Francisco: Harper and Row, 1990), 3.

our work that feeds the purpose of this book, we can identify three distinct characteristics of a missionary spirit.

First, the missionary spirit approaches ministry with more questions than answers. To embrace a #tentlife, one must ask *many* questions and allow oneself to live in wonder. In *Christianity Rediscovered*, Vincent Donavan recounts his life as a missionary in Africa. He quickly discovers that any personal preconceived thoughts about how his mission should run, including even direction from others, would not work well in his new setting. The missionary work could not be determined by him alone or by his community alone, but together they must listen and discern the completely new direction the Spirit was moving them toward.[14] This decision to let go of control takes great courage on the part of the missionary.

Courage to Move Away from "Always"

#Tentlife requires courage to do something new. One might wonder why this is needed. One might wonder why we can't simply keep doing what we have always done. We are in a new place, and yet we have not even moved. This challenge pertains to denominations as well as congregations. For example, suburban sprawl is catching up to many churches in rural North Carolina. The church has not moved location, but the land around it is filling with strip malls and housing developments. The way we have always done things isn't enough. Indeed, it's no secret that the old ways are only as old as the memory in the oldest members.

Crismons are the white ornaments in the shape of Christ symbols that a church will use to decorate a tree with during the season of Advent. I (Audrey) grew up with crismons on the tree in Naples,

---

14. Vincent J. Donavan, *Christianity Rediscovered* (Maryknoll, NY: Orbis, 2003) For examples of tent spaces inhabited by John Wesley, see Michael Beck with Jorge Acevedo, *Field Guide to Methodist Fresh Expressions* (Nashville, TN: Abingdon, 2020), pp. 24-25.

Florida. My first congregation did not have them and could not afford them. When I arrived at my current appointment and saw that they not only had crismons but they were also making more and people loved them, I was particularly excited. Although I love crismons I did not know much about them. I was caught off guard when someone asked me the date that the hanging of the crismons began. "Surely it was at least five hundred years ago," I responded. My response was so fast it made me question it, and so to find out the facts, I opened a web browser. To my surprise, the tradition I thought was most likely created in Europe during the early Reformation was actually created in the 1950s in the American Midwest. This was not the first time that my assumptions about something traditional were anachronistic. When a member or pastor tells me the church has always done something in a particular way, the word *always* usually means in the past five to ten years.

We are on a journey in our churches where the word *always* does not carry the weight it once did. Many have heard the phrase "if we always do what we've always done, we'll always get what we've always got." This phrase does not hold true for the church any longer. We continue to do what we have always done, yet we are not getting the same results we once got in the 1950s or 1960s. As much as one of the writers of this book loves felt-board Sunday school lessons, families no longer expect their children to be taught by them.

We are not the only institution that is experiencing these tensions. Some might remember a few years ago that the fast-food chain McDonald's was struggling. Old ways of bringing in more customers were no longer working. They could not do what they had always done. They made a major change, and they did so by listening to their people. Over the years, their biggest complaint was that breakfast hours did not last long enough in the morning. Finally, they listened to their customers and extended a majority of best-selling breakfast items all day, and their numbers increased.

The church is not selling sandwiches, but we can learn from the way in which McDonald's worked to get new results. They did not necessarily change their product or add new product, but they listened to needs around timing. We can't do what we've always done. We need to move in a new direction because we are no longer bearing enough fruit. It's delusional to think that if we do what we have always done with greater precision or excellence we will bear more fruit. Time to purchase a tent and pitch it out where the people are located. The time has come for us to evaluate honestly the function and space occupied by our properties.

Not only are people in our culture replacing church-sponsored spirituality with yoga and meditation at a local gym, even our sacred spaces are being replaced by a garden or funeral home. In most churches, even in downtown churches and cathedrals, there is no longer a need for a full-time wedding coordinator. People are getting married in parks, barns, and old factories. People are choosing to get married in the same location as their reception, where they can also partake in alcohol. Funeral services are often usurped by funeral homes who have not only expanded their viewing rooms but are now building on chapels and halls to host services and receptions in one location, to reduce (or pad) cost and time for their customers. To be honest, money is not the only driver for why people are opting for public rental spaces over private church spaces. The truth is that our church buildings have developed the reputation of being exclusive spaces. Not only are our old ways and old buildings not producing fruit, they have also become central to our narrative of exclusion. Over time this has happened in real ways and has also been exaggerated by the news media and social media, so that many people do not feel comfortable in a church building. And many have been told that they are not "worthy" of the buildings that represent our faith traditions. Stark evidence of this reality is clearly evident after one hundred years of conflict in Northern Ireland.

Strategy Session

Take time to work through these strategies with a small group of people from your church.

FAITH

Our faith helps us face the tough realities in our life, and our faith gives us hope enough to make the changes needed. Write down the tough realities about your church property.

In this chapter we identified that our properties can be both promise and problem. In which ways does your property make way for God's promises, and in what ways does it prove a problem to your overall mission?

MISSIONARY SPIRIT

A missionary spirit requires pastors to move out of their offices and join participants as they move into our community. How is your church encouraging the pastor to spend time? How many events does your church host that welcome and draw in the community?

A missionary spirit requires flexibility. How many spaces in your church are flexible and shared? Would you describe your church (people and property) as flexible? What is holding you back from being more flexible?

COURAGE TO MOVE AWAY FROM ALWAYS

List some things your church always does—and you don't know why they do it.

Are there some things you always do that you don't need to do anymore?

Are there some things you always do that can be changed or improved?

Chapter 2

#TempleLife

In the previous chapter about #tentlife, we encouraged churches to explore the stories, scriptures, and strategies that bring us back to our beginnings. Some readers and leaders might object, "Are you saying we should sell our churches and pitch tents everywhere?" Some leaders might answer, "Yes! Help us get out of our burdensome building."

The stories about #tentlife don't leave churches "homeless." The stories illuminate how a church can make space for others and resolve some of the burden of its building at the same time. You might ask further questions, such as: How does this space remain "holy"? Can a sanctuary be shared space? Some churches meeting in movie theaters, bars, and elementary schools might also ask: Why do we need cathedrals? Is there a purpose for dedicated space? Why do we even need religious symbols in the public square?

This chapter explores complex theological and philosophical questions concerning sacred space and religious property. If you are part of a community that has experienced transitioned church spaces or had your church space destroyed, you might know the layers of feeling associated with changing space. Although cradle-Christians were taught that "the church is a people," holy space and place are inseparable from religious experience—even for people who are done with church or others who are not interested in belonging to a faith community. Smells, memories, and feelings connected to a space tend to stick with us.

I (Audrey) have never been a member of a church that has not relocated or changed the space in a makeover. North Naples United Methodist Church, the church building of my childhood and youth, was sold, and the church purchased property a few miles away to expand. Cornerstone UMC, the church of my young adulthood, started in a school and moved into a building. First UMC of Lakeland, the church of my college years, experienced a tragic fire in its contemporary worship space. Branches United Methodist Church, my first appointment, burned down. And now First UMC of Miami, my current appointment, is being redeveloped.

Both Ken and I live in a state where various hurricanes have utterly destroyed sanctuaries. In each church that grieves, we remind people, "the church is a people." Yet, fifteen years after North Naples UMC was sold to the United Church of Christ, some of my childhood friends still insist on being married in the building where we grew up. Places hold space in our hearts. This is true particularly for religious space, because calling and vocation for ministry are always rooted in a place.[1]

Religious spaces are also signs to non-religious or wandering people. The world remembered its love for sacred space as millions watched the spire at Notre Dame burn. People in their thirties and forties, who claim not to be religious or spiritual, mourned the fire at Notre Dame. Though religious space does not hold weight in their world, the historical symbol of religion halfway around the world made them feel sorrow and dismay over its burning.

While many churches are anxious about how to keep their buildings open or might be considering a merger due to financial

---

1. See Randy G. Litchfield, *Roots and Routes: Calling, Ministry, and the Power of Place* (Nashville: Abingdon Press, 2019).

problems, one United Methodist church in the Midwest recently built a multi million-dollar sanctuary. Some ask why it did so. Here is that church's story.

Story—Church of the Resurrection

The story of the Church of the Resurrection (hereafter Resurrection) is familiar to most church leaders, because it is the largest United Methodist congregation. The church started as a "parachute drop" in a bedroom community on the Kansas territory outside Kansas City, Missouri. The church initiated its ministry in a funeral home with the pastor, his spouse, and a small team of volunteers. Nearly thirty years later, the church counts over twenty-five thousand members across its six campuses. From the funeral home, it moved to a high school gymnasium. During that time, many would ask when the church would build a sanctuary. The answer was always "Buildings are not our purpose. They are tools to help us fulfill Christ's mission. They are important tools, but only tools."[2] When it served more than six hundred in worship attendance, the church decided to buy land and build the first of many buildings on its property. Its first building was the Wesley Chapel, which members expected would be the church's permanent sanctuary. The physical building looks like a church, and definitely was a tool in aiding their mission. The first week when the congregation moved into its new sanctuary, their attendance doubled and never fell below one thousand after that. The congregation quickly outgrew their worship space. They needed a larger space.

Yet, since Resurrection was constantly growing, they decided to wait on building another permanent sanctuary and build what would eventually be their student center. The space was flexible and

---

2. Leawood Campus, Church of the Resurrection, "A Case for Building Our Permanent Sanctuary," July 19, 2011.

built with minimalist corporate architectural features. Religious symbols were also minimal since it would not be their permanent sanctuary. Once again, they outgrew the student center. For similar reasons recalled from the first building, they decided it was not yet time to build a permanent sanctuary. They were growing too fast and they did not want to build too small. The building committee decided to build the next building on their master plan and use that as a temporary sanctuary. They anticipated that the building would later be converted into a gymnasium. At this point in their story it appears that Resurrection, like the Israelites, would simply circle their property by setting up temporary worship spaces.

Finally, in 2011 the building team reconvened to explore the costs and purpose of building a permanent sanctuary structure. After much planning, dreaming, and praying, the building committee and leaders discerned—in spite of the church not having outgrown the current auditorium—that it was time to build the new sanctuary for the following reasons:

1. To have a dedicated and intentionally designed worship space to aid their mission by using the building as a tool to convene people in worship.

2. To provide space to shape those who dwell in them. The design of the permanent sanctuary accommodates both large and small services while maintaining an intimate feeling.

3. To build an iconic religious space in Kansas City that might foster a deeper sense of worship and an openness to encounters with God.[3]

When the Church of the Resurrection announced that it would be building this space, many critics scoffed at the expense and design,

---

3. Leawood Campus, "A Case for Building Our Permanent Sanctuary."

especially spent on a thirty-four-hundred-square-foot stained glass window. Some disciples, since the birth of the church, wonder why money is spent on ceremonial expenses when it could be spent on the poor or some other priority. Why was the Church of the Resurrection spending so much money on a sanctuary that contained ancient symbols and art such as stained glass and sculpture? The questions asked of Church of the Resurrection were also asked of other churches in America's largest cities during the twentieth century at the peak of Methodist urban growth and expansion. The answers to these questions reveal the motivations of a congregation and its leaders. The motivations for Church of the Resurrection leaders are two fold. First, to build a bigger and more intentional sanctuary where the space would shape those who worshipped within it. While seeker-driven megachurches (e.g., Willow Creek, which began as a high-school ministry, or Saddleback, which began in a massive California tent during the 1980s and 1990s) were minimizing barriers in sanctuaries (such as sculptures, crosses, and iconic art), the leaders at Resurrection discerned that younger generations preferred a revival of symbol, sacred space, and art. Thus, each piece of art at Resurrection is intentional, and its design tells a story.

Second, Resurrection wanted to provide a large symbol in the public square. This was the intent also of the great downtown churches in the late nineteenth and early twentieth centuries. The stained glass window wraps the west side of the sanctuary because that side faces the highway closest to the church. Anyone driving by can see the largest feature, a depiction of Jesus with his arms outstretched. The glass reflects Jesus giving the city a great big hug. There are many other symbols in Kansas City, and Resurrection wanted there to be a religious one as well.

The sacred symbol is only as strong as the authenticity of the people bearing the symbol. The sacred sites pertaining to the ministry of Jesus in Jerusalem continue to be sacred, even when we are unsure of the exact locations, because of what he did in those spaces. When Jesus walked on earth, he was the epitome of sacred space because he was God incarnate. His teaching, healing, and loving pointed to the authentic divine being within him. In Jesus, God becomes local. Jesus came and was God. He pointed people to God and the worship of God.

Our churches are this body of Christ, and most of the time we point and lead to the worship of God as experienced in a church building. Yet, the sacred space is a strong and authentic symbol when the church is also outside of the building and fulfilling the authentic ministry of Christ. In her article, "Can We Talk about a Theology of Sacred Space?" Susan White describes it in this way,

Just as there was a necessary locatedness to the ministry of Jesus, that his life of healing, teaching, preaching, and forgiving was identified and attached to certain particular places and that those places derived their sacred significance from the action performed there, the same is true with the church. There is a necessary locatedness about its ministry as well. There are places attached to its life of healing, teaching, preaching, forgiving, and the sacred significance of those places is wholly dependent on the dominical authenticity of that ministry.[4]

The symbol of a giant Jesus hugging Kansas City becomes as strong as the ways in which the people at Church of the Resurrection hug its city. Their giant building, which cost a lot of money, holds them accountable to proclaim and live out the commitment expressed in the symbol they broadcast. Although Church of the Resurrection is known nationally in the Christian community, it is known intimately in the community where it is located. Church of the Resurrection is constantly giving its city a hug.

---

4. Susan White, "Can We Talk about a Theology of Sacred Space?" in *Searching for Sacred Space*, ed. John Runkle (New York: Church Publishing, Inc., 2002), 29.

Scripture and Theology

Church of the Resurrection is not the first to wrestle with the questions of church building cost and use, nor the first to cause others to wrestle with these questions. Mircea Eliade's book *The Sacred and the Profane* explores these questions about space, ritual, and religious life. Eliade argues that space is not homogenous, meaning that spaces are not all equally the same. We notice this separation when we step over a threshold that separates two spaces. Or in another sign of separation, notice Moses removing his shoes when he realizes that he is standing on holy ground. Or consider Jacob's dream at Haran, in which he perceives God's messengers going up and down a ladder. When Jacob wakes up, he understands that his resting place is holy land, and he calls it "Bethel," which means "house of God."[5]

Eliade observes that God's spiritual presence is transubstantiated (made physically present) in a holy site, and the holy site is determined by God. At the holy site a break occurs between the profane and sacred, because divine presence descends, ascends, and communicates at that specific site. Space becomes sacred when God's presence inhabits the *substance* of the sacred space.

Jonathan Smith, in *To Take Place*, observes that sacred space is *situational* rather than substantive. Smith thinks sacred space is not defined by a divine power authorizing it as sacred. Instead, an event happens at a site, and then it is memorialized. "Memorial" seems to characterize many sacred sites in Israel, including sites that are specific to the life of Jesus. When Jesus fed five thousand, the location was not ordained space, but it was simply the space where they stopped along the way. Years later people return to this place. Believers do not simply return to it, but they treat it differently. People might even behave differently at the site. Smith goes so far as to use the example of the temple in Jerusalem. He states that there is "no

---

5. Mircea Eliade, *The Sacred and the Profane: The Nature of Religion* (New York: Harcourt Publishing, 1957), 27.

inherent location" for the temple.[6] God did not ordain the space for the temple, it was chosen. So, what makes it sacred?

For Smith, a space is sacred because of what happens in the space, how it is treated, and the behavior that occurs within the space. Jeanne Hilde agrees: "places are sacred because they are made so by human beings."[7] Many faith communities behave this way. The property purchased to build a church is typically selected by a committee with business knowledge. For example, the Church of the Resurrection started because a new-church development committee used population statistics to determine where people were moving. They expected the largest growth in the greater Kansas City area. Yet even a funeral home was selected temporarily to celebrate the Resurrection each week. From Eliade's point of view, the symbolism of death and resurrection (Christ) was physically present in that funeral home. From Smith's point of view, the space became sacred because of what was happening functionally inside it.

In the first chapter we focused on the earliest form of worship space, the meeting tent. The people of God in their tribes met and encountered God in the meeting tent for more than two hundred years. As God's people in their tribes became established in the land, they sought a monarchy to consolidate power with a king to rule over the tribal territories. Kings and other rulers tend to be institution builders, and they establish palaces to symbolize and memorialize their authority. Though not everyone in Israel, according to Deuteronomy and 1 Samuel, supported a monarchy, physical, permanent structures were sought and built. King David was apparently the first who dreamed about building a temple in Jerusalem. David gave much of his fortune to the future temple and drafted the plans for it. Yet, like Moses with the promised land, he would not be the one to build it. Due to David's lust, God chose David and

---

6. Jonathan Z. Smith, *To Take Place: Toward Theory in Ritual* (Chicago: The University of Chicago Press, 1987), 83.

7. Jeanne Halgren Hilde, *Sacred Power, Sacred Space: An Introduction to Christian Architecture and Worship* (New York: Oxford University Press, 2008), 7.

Bathsheba's son, Solomon, to build the temple. The temple stood for four hundred years.

The temple would be destroyed in 587 BCE. The temple was rebuilt when exiles returned, but without the physical temple, the sacrificial system was suspended. For those driven into exile, with no chance of return, their faith practices during the Greek empire moved into synagogues. The word *synagogue* comes from the Greek translation of the Hebrew Bible and is composed of two words. The first word is *syn*, which means "to join." The second word is *gogeo*, which means "to gather." So, in English, the Greek word *synagogue* means "coming together." The word *synagogue* is a verb that became a noun. The "coming together" included singing, praying, reading from the Torah scrolls, a teaching by the Levites, and more singing. Jews and Christians continue these practices when we gather today!

The exile mostly dispersed the leaders in Judah, and when they returned seventy years later, the people rebuilt their homes and eventually rebuilt the temple, which stood and was maintained for nearly five hundred years. The second temple built by Zerubbabel was not described in terms as grand as Solomon's, but its purpose, established through the sacrificial system, sustained a gathering space for righteous people to learn and worship and meet God. The temple as a physical center for God's presence was important for people of faith.

We see the central role of sacred space, even with the massive replacement and expansion of the temple by the corrupt King Herod a few years prior to the birth of Jesus. In Luke 2:22-40 we read that Mary and Joseph take Jesus to the temple to be presented to the Lord as taught in the Law from Moses. Upon their arrival, they encounter Simeon who was guided by the Spirit to the temple. Simeon prophesied about Jesus, and scripture says that Mary and Joseph were amazed by the things Simeon was saying about their son. On the same occasion, Anna (an eighty-four-year-old prophetess) spent day and night in the temple, fasting and praying. She too recognized Jesus as God and began worshipping him. Jesus's consecration for mission did not take place in a garden or at the lake but occurred as expected in the temple.

Immediately after telling the presentation story about Jesus, we see the only other childhood story about Jesus. Luke 2:41-52 recounts Jesus's time in the temple when he was teaching and preaching as a young boy. His parents took the young Jesus and their entire family to Jerusalem for the Festival of the Passover. When the family leaves, Jesus stays behind in Jerusalem. Mary and Joseph did not realize for a day that they left him, assuming he was in another caravan. The worried parents return to Jerusalem, and after three days of looking find him in the temple.

> When his parents see him, they're shocked. His mother says, "Child, why have you treated us like this? Listen! Your father and I have been worried. We've been looking for you!"
> Jesus replies, "Why were you looking for me? Didn't you know that it was necessary for me to be in my Father's house?" But they didn't understand what he said to them. (Luke 2:48-50 CEB)

Jesus describes the temple as "his Father's house." Jesus claims that the temple is God's dwelling place, which places great importance on the temple.

In chapter 3, we will explore Jesus's concern for the temple as seen in John's story of "cleansing the temple." Since he was born, Jesus did not have a place to lay his head. As the anticipated Messiah, the Christ, he understood the importance and place of the temple for God's people.

In John's Gospel, written approximately thirty years after the destruction of the second temple (70 CE) by the Romans, we read the story of Jesus cleansing the temple. The story is told to John's community after the early Christians separated from Jewish institutions, including the synagogues. In this story, Jesus compares his body to the temple.

Jesus answered, "Destroy this temple and in three days I'll raise it up."

The Jewish leaders replied, "It took forty-six years to build this temple, and you will raise it up in three days? But the temple Jesus was talking about was his body. After he was raised from the dead, his disciples remembered what he had said, and they believed the scripture and the word that Jesus had spoken. (John 2:19-22 CEB)

By 100 CE, the early Christians understood Jesus's anger toward corruption in the demolished Jerusalem temple as a sign of his death and resurrection. They realized that Jesus was pointing to his body, understood by Paul as the "body of Christ," which for Christians becomes the replacement for the temple. In this revelation of Jesus as God's Son, the claim would be used against him when he was on trial by the Sanhedrin.[8]

In the New Testament letters to various early Christian churches, prior to John's Gospel, Paul invites his readers to understand their own bodies as temples. He writes to the Corinthians, "Don't you know that your body is a temple of the Holy Spirit who is in you? Don't you know that you have the Holy Spirit from God, and you don't belong to yourselves? You have been bought and paid for, so honor God with your body" (1 Cor 6:19-20 CEB). In his letter to the Corinthians Paul enhances this analogy by imploring readers that their bodies are not only temples of the Lord but also together form the body of Christ. Collectively, as a faith community, we also are temples.

Through the Hebrew Bible understanding of temple and synagogue, and through the life and teaching of Jesus and his apostles, we see that our relationship with physical church buildings is both physical and spiritual. A healthy view of church property embraces the idea that sacred space is useful yet also transcended by the collective body of Christ when fulfilling God's mission in a local community. From the beginning to the end of scripture we see that place

---

8.   Mark 14:58.

and space for the worship of God is important. Large temples stood as physical symbols of the indwelling spiritual presence of God with a people. Even Rome embraced the temple and its symbolism—Hadrian tried to place his statue in a temple to the god Jupiter, built on top of the ruined Jerusalem temple—when it benefited Rome to do so. The Roman government also saw and appreciated the ways in which the temple and the faith that embraced it provided laws and values that helped create a healthy and civil society.

Strategy

So, in light of the shift over the centuries from impressive temples to mobile and modest faith communities, why do we need cathedrals? Why do we need expensive church buildings? Throughout Jewish and Christian history, especially after the destruction of the Jerusalem temple, faith communities out of necessity have spread and worshipped without the burden of property. Some Christians might answer, "We don't need them. We can worship in a park or at home with a small group of people and a guitar." We who are committed people of faith probably do not *need* the buildings for ourselves, but for those who do not yet experience faithfulness and discipleship, we need sacred spaces as symbols of faith in our community. The cathedral is not necessarily built for those who are in it but for those who will come to know faith through it and those whose minds and hearts will be lifted due to the scope of its message. As we contemplate building new buildings, maintaining old ones, and redeveloping properties, we adapt our strategy to plan for those already in our spaces as well as those who have not yet oriented their life to the body of Christ. *The church and its buildings exist for those already inside and those who are* not *yet inside and may never be.*

In *The Naked Public Square*, Richard John Neuhaus writes about the continued need for physical and verbal forms of faith in society. Our country was formed by people seeking freedom to practice their faith. Our democratic forms of government were shaped by Judeo-Christian teaching and Greek city-state traditions. These traditions shaped what we believed and how laws and societies are ordered. Physical churches, synagogues, and mosques contribute to the public square as symbols of our shared values—or so we hope and pray. If these religious traditions and their physical symbols lose their salt and light, "politics becomes civil war carried on by other means."[9]

Thanks to digital technology on screens, we see many symbols each day. Americans typically see four thousand to ten thousand images per day, and the images we see influence what we buy, which in many ways reveals what we care about.[10] Our steeples and crosses and stars are among the public symbols seen on a daily basis—as long as they are still present. In part, this is the purpose for the steeple that rises above the skyline and draws attention by ringing chimes or bells.

A cathedral or a modest church building becomes part of the public square if it opens itself up to the public and reaches out beyond the walls into the public. To maintain buildings and justify the cost in building, *our sanctuaries can be holy space and human space.* We see this when our churches serve as polling stations during elections. This is the reality necessary for many buildings today. The challenge comes from trying to maintain the sacred symbolism among the public in a culture that is fragmented and segmented by thousands of competing messages and symbols.

As our culture became more competitive and consumer driven, it became harder to find a balance between work and life. The digital natives among younger generations are moving away from the term

9. Richard John Neuhaus, *The Naked Public Square: Religion and Democracy in America* (Grand Rapids, MI: Eerdmans, 1984), 21.

10. Joe Simpson, "Finding Brand Success in the Digital World," *Forbes*, August 25, 2017, https://www.forbes.com/sites/forbesagencycouncil/2017/08/25/finding-brand-success-in-the-digital-world/#41e1d05a626e.

balance and moving toward a work/life *blend.*[11] Work and life blend together. Work space and life space blend together as more people work from home. Work spaces are now being transformed to include sofas and stand-up desks with treadmills under them. The bifurcation (separation) of space and time is blending as a symphony. Ryan Jenkins, a life coach, writes:

> Stop thinking your life needs to be "balanced." Balance implies things need to be of equal relation in order to reach success. I believe your life from birth to death should be thought of as a symphony. A great symphony is played with many different types of instruments and each played at different levels of intensity at different times during the performance. Your commitments, just like instruments in a symphony, need to be adjusted to whatever is most important at that point in time. The goal is not to have work-life balance. It is to have work-life harmony.[12]

This shift in how we disorder and blend our lives, in terms of time, space, and titles, is affecting how we practice our faith. Worship is not restricted to a physical building, and yoga is not restricted to a yoga studio, but is now also practiced in some churches. So, for the existing church building to maintain its space it must blend holy time and human time. Cathedrals can be open. New sanctuaries can be designed as dedicated space and flexible space. Our culture today does not restrict holy space and holy time to a fixed hour on Sunday morning or Wednesday evening. So, if we are going to spend time, money, and talents on holy space, it must sustain a variety of purposes.

---

11. "Generation Y: Work Life Blend," *Company Match News*, April 4, 2018, https://www.companymatch.me/news/english/generation-y-work-life-blend/.

12. Ryan Jenkins, "5 Ways Millennials Are Redefining Work-Life Balance," *Inc.*, February 5, 2018, https://www.inc.com/ryan-jenkins/this-is-how-millennials-view-work-life-balance.

Ownership

While church members from First United Methodist Church, Miami, were discerning what to do with a downtown church building, many asked why we would be building a physical structure and spending so much money on it. A retired pastor answered with a story he told about a small impoverished town in Central America. The town slowly became a city, so many people felt they needed a church building. Over time, the people in the community raised the funds and partnered with a denomination to build a great church building. After the building was complete, some would visit the town and ask community members why they built the church when so many in the town were so poor. The community members often answered by saying that the church was their hope and joy because it was not just the property of one denomination or another, but it was the church for the whole community. That church belonged to everyone.

This desire is shared when building any cathedral. In fact, church members don't own the church building. Trustees don't own the building. Pastors certainly don't own the church buildings, nor should they. In the best of cases a church and a community understand that the building belongs to them and that they too belong to the building. This "presence" is why everyone mourned when the Paris Cathedral of Notre Dame burned.

In Miami, I (Audrey) pass by two Catholic churches on my bike ride to work. Both have large statues of Jesus in front. One of the churches is in the very wealthy financial district of Miami and the other is in the hustling heart of downtown Miami. No matter what time of day it is, I am likely to see men and women and children of all ages standing in front of the large structure with their hands in Jesus's hands, praying. The people touch that symbol and believe that Jesus is there for them. They believe that this sacred space is activated just for them.

The mystery of holy space is that it can take root on a street corner or in a sanctuary pew. A place is not intrinsically holy because it has walls. It is holy because a people share a common purpose for living life as disciples.

As stewards of holy space, whether tent or temple, we are accountable for whether the space transforms the people inside of it and beyond the four walls. The emphasis is not so much on what makes the space holy, as whether it leaves those who enter it with a new window to interpret the world as holy. Thomas Merton writes about how to see the world and those around us as holy:

> In Louisville, at the corner of Fourth and Walnut, in the center of the shopping district, I was suddenly overwhelmed with the realization that I loved all these people, that they were mine and I theirs, that we could not be alien to one another even though we were total strangers. It was like waking from a dream of separateness, of spurious self-isolation in a special world. . . . This sense of liberation from an illusory difference was such a relief and such a joy to me that I almost laughed out loud. . . . I have the immense joy of being man, a member of a race in which God Himself became incarnate. As if the sorrows and stupidities of the human condition could overwhelm me, now that I realize what we all are. And if only everybody could realize this! But it cannot be explained. There is no way of telling people that they are all walking around shining like the sun.[13]

When we encounter God in the temple, we are being trained to perceive the image of God in every person. "The LORD is my light and my salvation. Should I fear anyone?" (Ps 27:1 CEB). The light that dwells in the gathered body of Christ is present also in the world. Temple life teaches us about the permeability of holy space and human space. The bread of the Eucharist and the water of baptism are outward and visible signs of grace, and yet they are elements coming

---

13. Thomas Merton, *Conjectures of a Guilty Bystander* (New York: Doubleday & Company, 1966), 156.

from the earth and carried into the temple as offerings in response to the divine gift of life. The ordinary person we encounter in the other is not a danger or threat. Instead, he or she is walking around, shining like the sun, awaiting the stranger who will become a neighbor or friend. And this has become possible as God, who is wholly other, pitches a tent in our neighborhood and calls us to share life together as friends.

Strategy Session

Where have you experienced holy ground?

What made this ground holy for you?

Can you think of an area in your church's space that seems extravagant or controversial?

Some readers might recall the Christian chorus *Sanctuary*. "Lord prepare me, to be a Sanctuary." How does your sacred space provide room for both holy and human experiences? How does your body provide sacred space for experiencing God's presence?

How does your temple exist for those outside its wall?

Chapter 3

#MuseumLife

Museums are places that support memory and remembering. Whether an art museum, science museum, or history museum, each works toward the goal of preservation. A museum is "an institution that cares for (conserves) a collection of artifacts and other objects of artistic, cultural, historical, or scientific importance."[1] Over the years, museums have expanded their understanding of themselves. Preservation and memory are important values for museums. To overcome the disinterest and lack of revenue in a facility full of fossils, and to be a place that fosters education and learning and growing, many museums now also focus on imagination and innovation. In addition to past inventions, art, and sculptures, museums also highlight future technology and art forms. Museums now include large cafes and gift shops, which at times are larger than the actual museum. Museums open their doors to the public by providing free weekly admission days and affordable annual passes. They understand that community outreach must be a value and top priority.

Museum directors and boards dance a delicate balance between preserving and conserving the artifacts and engaging the people. Not only are the directors tasked with preserving and conserving

---

1. "Museum," *Wikipedia*, https://en.wikipedia.org/wiki/Museum, accessed June 15, 2020.

artifacts but also the buildings they inhabit since many museums are historical sites in our larger cities. In describing the work of a museum and its staff, some church leaders recognize similarities to "Old First Church... found in the downtown district . . . there are often various Old First Churches representing deferent denominations. Old First Church is easily recognized by its building, which speaks to the architecture of its time. Its steeple was part of the city skyscape before the skyscrapers and strip malls rose around it. Old First Church is more than a landmark, but it is a symbol of its denomination in the city.[2]

In this chapter we will explore some common stories and themes among "First Churches" in towns, county seats, and urban city-centers. We will search scripture for lessons and work through basic strategies to assist churches in discerning their next steps.

Story—The "Old First Church"

Both writers have worked in "Old First Churches" in metropolitan cities as well as in smaller towns. As we compared notes with each other and with other pastors similarly placed, some common themes affect the life of "Old First Church" concerning property, bureaucracy, and nostalgia.

Upon visiting another First Church in Florida, the pastor and a few leaders gave us (visiting pastor and leaders) a tour of their facility. They showed us the usual "First Church" spaces, such as the very fancy parlor, the dedicated bridal room, the sanctuary, the chapel, the library, the wall of paintings or pictures of pastors past, the archives room, and to our surprise they showed us a space we thought was only particular to our "First Church": the ceramics room. Their

---

2. Ezra Earl Jones and Robert Wilson, *What's Next for Old First Church* (New York: Harper & Row, 1974), 1.

particular ceramics room was full of two kilns, prefabricated clay molds, and dried-out tubes of paint. The visitors looked at one another and started laughing, and then the church leaders from the church we were visiting joined us in laughing. We shared with them the story of our ceramics room.

The ceramics room at FUMC Miami was given by and dedicated for a faithful disciple of Christ from our church. This woman loved ceramics. She would host ceramics classes where people came to the church and learned how to paint and mold bowls. The ceramics room was also part of another ministry the church started with the elderly. Each day eighty to one hundred retirees would come to the church for lunch and activities such as Bible study and ceramics. The volunteers made ceramics for themselves and to give away. The pieces were also sold at times to help move forward the mission of the church. The program engaged many seniors from the government apartment buildings near the church. The seniors typically did not come to church on Sunday, but in many ways their daily lunch, fellowship, learning, and service was church for them. It was how they encountered Christ. There was one paid staff person for the program, and the rest of the leaders were church members who volunteered their time. In many ways the senior program and the ceramics room were Fresh Expressions long before we ever heard the phrase.

The program ran strong until some of the key leaders passed away, moved away, or retired. Soon the group became smaller, the church became smaller, and funds to run it became smaller. The program was soon taken over by the City of Miami, and the relationship between the church and program also faded. Due to financial gifts, an entire dedicated space was given to one person. The passion she had for seniors and ceramics was not passed on to the next generation. Thirty years later, many pastors in Old First Churches are left with closets of cat figurine molds and dry paint—afraid to throw them away lest they be scolded. Our story at First Miami was not different from the story of the church we went to visit. Pastors and parishioners alike did not know what to do with the space or the stuff within it. In some ways, we felt a bit paralyzed by the past property and the nostalgia carried with it.

The ceramics room or the archives room or whatever room is full of artifacts from ministry in the past is a symbolic status for the property that many "Old First Churches" inherited. Pastors and church leaders cannot necessarily use the inheritance in tangible ways for Fresh Expressions of ministry. Cynthia Weems compares this dilemma to china that her grandmother gave to her. Her grandmother gave it to her before she was married, concerned that she would not marry. It was very important for her grandmother to give it to her. She received the china with gratitude and grace. Years later she reflected on her china set and realized a few regrets: she only used the china on holidays. Her daughter, who would inherit the china, thought it was interesting and pretty but not useful or practical.[3]

"Old First Churches" understand these regrets about their property: people visit during special occasions and holidays, and younger members of the church believe the buildings are interesting but not necessarily useful or practical. Many younger generations are also dealing with the reality of a building falling apart. During a church conference, one colleague from South Carolina had to step out and take a call. A few minutes later, I also had to step out and take a call. At lunch we learned that both of us responded to the giant leak and subsequent flood in the women's bathroom in our respective choir rooms. Pastors in First Churches (and most other leaders in aging structures) can add property management to their list of skills, since many spend at least 10 percent of their time putting out property "fires," especially if the fire is caused by an eighty-year-old electrical system.

Property is not the only story at "Old First Church." Many First Church pastors tell stories about the extreme bureaucracy in long-established churches. The announcement section of the bulletin often lists committee meetings on the church schedule. Many churches with fifty people in worship attendance operate with nine committees. With few funds, reduced budgets, shrinking numbers in worship, and overwhelming building problems, churches are often forced to look inward, which stunts their growth and outreach. The cycle continues and even causes great anxiety and stress in a congregation, which breeds the need to control. The need for control and power in times where a congregation feels out of control and powerless plays out in its committees.

Termites are an awful scourge in southern Florida. Termites can infest pipe organs and sanctuary space and also outdoor bulletin boards. At one of the churches I (Audrey) was serving, the pesky wood lovers got into a bulletin board until it desperately needed replacing. The replacement cost was high, however, because the bulletin board had a wood and plexiglass case around it with a lock on it—so no one would steal the much-loved pictures from church events. The key had been lost for at least ten years. One might expect the conversation about the replacement would be an easy ten-minute agenda item, especially since one member indicated before the meeting the board should be replaced with a TV and offered to pay for it. The trustees meeting soon resembled an episode from the TV show *The Office*. Detailed conversations about how one gets pictures on screens from cameras ensued. The details were followed by a grand debate about using digital media and getting permission from parents as it could be digital and not paper pictures being displayed. For the moment, the generous, new, young member regretted joining the committee and wondered if he had made the right decision in being part of a church to begin with. After an hour-and-a-half-long discussion, the committee approved the TV, and all left the meeting dissatisfied and probably more confused about digital media altogether. The work of committees becomes even more difficult for a First Church that is located in a major metropolitan city. Most members live in the suburbs and drive into the church. Due to traffic and timing, meetings during the week are hard to schedule. Meetings are then held on Sunday and encroach on the spirit of the Sabbath. Members come to worship, but they also come to attend a meeting and do business. A colleague, who is a First Presbyterian Church pastor, described his frustration with engaging leaders during the week. Meetings were only held on Sundays, which at times killed the impact of the overall worship experience. Worship became a side thing and not the main thing on a Sunday. Death by committee is a reality, and it also has the power to kill the worship experience if constantly held on Sundays. Some churches have been successful in reducing committees by using technology to overcome distance and traffic. It's during hard conversations on committees when the discouraging words of First Church charter members are heard: "If only we could go back to how things used to be."

The 1950s and early 1960s were (allegedly) the glory years of many Old First Churches. Nostalgia is a common theme in many First Churches and probably many other churches. As churches decline, members find peace and comfort in remembering the "good old days" when the sanctuaries were packed, and young women vied for the coveted position of education chair. A certain honor is shared among members of a past generation who shared in the wonder years of Old First Church. Unfortunately, it is easy to get caught up in the honor and forget the fault lines that were also part of the history of First Churches. Many cities and towns had not one First Church but two. One First Church was aligned with more progressive commitments to abolish slavery, and the other was desperate to conserve a way of life. Neither First Church had African Americans in worship. While the glory days included large choirs and overflowing Sunday schools, they also included alliances with the KKK and other pro-segregation efforts.

One retired pastor shared a story of his experience as a young pastor at a First Church in Tennessee, his home state. It was the late 1960s and desegregation was beginning in some larger cities. As worship was about to begin, the pastor saw a young African American family walk in the doors of the church. The usher, a white man, looked confused and frustrated. The pastor noticed it was taking way too long for the usher to seat the family. After a few more minutes the usher came up to the pastor, sweating and flustered. He asked the pastor if they should be allowed in the church and if so, where they should sit. The pastor responded, "They are allowed in this church and you can sit them right up here in the front row next to my family."

"Old First Churches" try to survive or thrive in ever-changing and complex social settings. Although the downtown church could at one time choose to turn away people because of color, race, class, or sexual orientation, many of them learned they would need to open their doors wider between 1970 and 1990. By this time many progressive and conservative First Churches merged and became more open. The people moving into the downtown square were very different from their charter members, and some First Churches did a great job in welcoming them. Homeless ministries became common in First Churches. Many First Churches also became pioneers in welcoming other groups and nonprofit service providers to occupy their space. Downtown parking lots produced big money for the First Church and became a large percentage of the annual revenue for the church. Over time, many First Church pastors admit to renting closet space to bring in revenue to keep the building afloat. Due to space restrictions from renters and partners, church programing declined and took second priority to the renters. Many churches with a day care meeting in the education classrooms are familiar with this tension. Pastors, like museum directors, dance the dance of keeping the property maintained while at the same time keeping the people engaged. In frustrating moments, some church leaders wonder whether we are turning the temple into a house of wolves.

Scripture

When we turn to scripture, we find that pastors and parishioners are not the only ones to become frustrated with church property. Think back to a vexed reaction in the church building when something important and expensive broke, such as an elevator or a boiler. We tend to act out our anxiety in these circumstances.

Sacred space and the proper use of the temple courts provide the context for the only time we see Jesus angry and upset to the point of getting out a whip. The outburst, which is described in all four Gospels, is probably a key reason why the Sanhedrin put Jesus on trial.

In the previous chapter on #templelife we explored the destruction of the temple as a symbol of death and resurrection. In this chapter we will look more fully at why the money changers were such a problem. This part of the text reads:

> It was nearly time for the Jewish Passover, and Jesus went up to Jerusalem. He found in the temple those who were selling cattle, sheep, and doves, as well as those involved in exchanging currency sitting there. He made a whip from ropes and chased them all out of the temple, including the cattle and the sheep. He scattered the coins and overturned the tables of those who exchanged currency. He said to the dove sellers, "Get these things out of here! Don't make my Father's house a place of business." (John 2:13-16 CEB)

Jesus makes his way to Jerusalem as Passover is drawing near. When he arrives at the temple, he finds a commercial marketplace. People are selling cattle, sheep, and doves. Jesus specifically drives out the cattle and the sheep. The sheep and cattle were sold inside the temple court for pilgrims like Jesus. Sojourners making their way from distant territory for Passover found it impractical to bring their live animals to sacrifice. So, a market system emerged with the participation, and to the benefit, of the temple authorities. For business opportunists, this solution to a practical problem seems like a great way to keep pilgrims satisfied, forgiveness and reconciliation possible, and the ministry of sacrifice funded. However, the accommodation is condemned by Jesus.

Money changing also provided a practical solution for pilgrims. Money changers sat outside the temple gates and would exchange coins with the emperor's face on them for blank coins, which were acceptable for the temple tax. Money changers apparently were charging an exchange fee, and at times were gouging the people, especially around high holy days such as Passover. The account in Matthew 21:13 says, "He said to them, 'It's written, *My house will be called a house of prayer.* But you've made it a hideout for crooks'" (Matt 21:13 CEB). In a generous commentary on the situation, Rev. Paul Shupe writes, "More than likely, all involved had simply settled into comfortable behaviors that enabled them to meet institutional goals, turning an increasingly blind eye to the unsavory possibilities of corruption inherent in changing money."[4]

Our "First Churches" don't sell animals in our parking lots, which are then butchered on the altar in forgiveness of sins. Even though online giving apps take a percentage for automatically managing the accounting and banking, these money changers aren't

---

4. Paul Shupe, "Third Sunday in Lent," in *Feasting on the Word: Year B, Volume 2* (Louisville: Westminster John Knox Press, 2008), 94.

taking advantage of personal worship obligations and reconciliation. Although our churches don't struggle with the identical issues Jesus confronted in the Jerusalem temple, we still live with the tension of keeping the "museum" open while at the same time maintaining the original purpose of the sacred space. We struggle with questions like, How much time and space do we rent or give to outside groups and still keep our programing faithful and true? How do we determine who we rent space to? How do we stay faithful to our call to hospitality and maintain holy space in the heart of our towns and cities?

Strategies

Each church manages different issues pertaining to finances, property and people, but some common themes and strategies help churches come closer to being faithful and fruitful in complex settings. One typical group that churches welcome are the unhoused populations in our cities. Due to the long-standing partnerships churches nurture over the years, they are some of the first organizations called upon to help in housing, feeding, and providing services for the homeless. Around the world, due to massive repression and famine, refugees are another group finding help and healing in city-center churches. In many cities, churches are offering sanctuary to undocumented immigrants. For many pastors and followers of Jesus, one of the primary reasons the church exists is to offer sanctuary, which justifies the purpose of the sacred space. Yet when we engage in the incarnational ministry of Christ and when our buildings put on the body of Christ, consensus becomes very complex. In *Life Together*, Dietrich Bonhoeffer reminds us that our idea of community is often more beloved than it is actually lived out.[5] Opening our doors requires strong and spiritual leadership.

Strong and Spiritual Leadership

I (Ken) served a large city-center congregation (Providence UMC in Charlotte, North Carolina). One of the most important spaces was a living area where families experiencing homelessness lived and slept. On average twenty persons were there at a given time and hundreds of people in the church spent some time each year serving alongside them. This could involve spending the night, preparing breakfast or dinner, driving individuals to medical appointments or job interviews, or simply engaging in conversation. The relationships were mutually beneficial, in that there was giving and receiving among all. One member of the church told me that her perception of persons experiencing homelessness was transformed as she would watch a young man iron his work uniform and leave very early in the morning each day to serve in a nearby restaurant.

This ministry space within our congregation had complex usage. The church had an extensive ministry with children, including day programs with their families. Sometimes the confluence of these two communities—persons experiencing homelessness and parents of young children with an appropriate desire for safety—would spark conflict. The ministry space was a place of safety and refuge for these two communities, and my role at times was to listen, mediate, and interpret.

The meeting place is never a space for the benefit of any one constituency. A house of prayer for all people inevitably brings together people in their differences. A mature spiritual journey draws us into sacred space, where we meet God who loves and cares for us. Here, God teaches us to create hospitable space for those whose lives are

---

5. Dietrich Bonhoeffer, *Life Together*, trans. John W. Doberstein (New York: Harper & Row, 1954).

different from ours. Strong spiritual leadership is required for staff and participants to live with the complexity, to problem-solve as necessary, and to point people back to the mission and call of Christ. A homeless ministry and a church school can live together as incredible partners.

Partners and Collaborators

Where Old First Church is declining in membership, and committee fatigue sets in, it is hard to imagine any kind of ministry starting on its own. Even churches with large administrative structures struggle to properly house and feed persons experiencing homelessness and offer services to the community. Sometimes after opening their doors to the community, the First Church realizes they have bitten off more than they can chew. For example, in 2008 while the US was experiencing the worst financial crisis in decades, the country of South Africa was experiencing its own crisis as a massive wave of refugees migrated from Zimbabwe into South Africa. Political and economic conflict led to food shortages, and hundreds of thousands of Zimbabweans flooded into South Africa. This set the stage for the church to be the church and open its doors to provide shelter, food, and water.

Many churches did open their doors and provide resources. Some worked with fifty people or twenty-five people, depending on their capacity and the need in their community. Central Methodist Mission of Johannesburg housed five hundred people. Refugees slept in hallways, classrooms, and closets. The efforts were led by Pastor Paul Verryn. The church soon became a small city with weekly meetings about governance and cleaning. This hospitality occurred in a city, and nation, that had mixed feeling about the refugees. Fear of the immigrants became a crisis as the refugees poured into the country. Impoverished citizens of South Africa worried about the refugees taking their jobs, because the newcomers would accept less pay.

And thus, the news media coverage of Central Methodist Mission was not balanced. Some journalists and observers were disgusted

with the church's efforts due to politics, and others in the community felt it was not fair to let refugees compromise their church buildings. The historic church building did suffer from the presence of the
refugees. Old plumbing systems were often breaking. When the crisis subsided, the church property suffered many bumps and bruises.
The building is still standing and being renovated. The damage done
could have been much worse. Central Methodist Mission and other
churches in South Africa were able to keep their doors open to the
refugees and maintain their facilities by not doing it alone. Five or six
other organizations worked with the church to manage the refugee
residents and manage the public health concerns of so many people
living in such close quarters. Their partners knew better than the
church how to host and house large groups of people.

This lesson about capacity, learned from a crisis in Africa, is instructive for US church leaders. We need to know our own capacity
and know when to ask for help. Many churches can manage a feeding
program, but when a church steps out to provide a warm place for
persons experiencing homelessness during the cold winter, it ought
to consider reaching out to a partner. Partnerships and professionals
who have more experience in working with a certain group help pro-
tect both the guest and the church. The last thing a Christian wants
to do is harm someone while making the effort to help him or her.
Our society is very litigious, and the liability when churches help is
high. First Churches are often the heart and conscience of the city, so
they must lead in hospitality and risk-taking mission. Fewer mistakes
are made when churches include other partners in their efforts.

Staying Ahead of the Wave

Surfing is popular on some Florida beaches. In surfing, when
one catches a wave, the surfer doesn't start on top of the wave or
behind the wave. Riding a wave starts ahead of the swelling water.
By analogy, Old First Church can stay afloat and get momentum by

positioning the church ahead of the waves that can either sink us or save us. Most First Churches are located on property with high land value. However, most First Churches are fragile and declining with aging adults passing away. Unless the leaders can get ahead of the wave, fragile Old First Churches will fall and flounder.

A defining factor for First Church's future is the "particular moment in which a congregation decides to act."[6] In 1974, urban decay and poverty spread in the center of cities and towns, which often include more than one First Church. Some cities have deteriorated further, and many town squares are now boarded and empty. But other cities and some towns within driving distance of a city are experiencing renewal, if not a building boom, as millennials relocate to walkable cities. "Some congregations have pursued yesterday for so long that they no longer have the resources to change direction or engage in expanded, different ministries that would bring new people and new life to their churches."[7]

We find ourselves waiting on the back end of the wave ridden by past generations. We are looking at the back end of the wave so intently that we can't watch for the next wave that God wants us to ride. In many congregations, participation dwindles to the point that the church simply maintains what it has. For Old First Church to survive, it must seize the moment to make some tough decisions about its mission, its adaptive mindset, and its future.

Stay Flexible

I (Ken) came to a new understanding of adaptation a few years ago when I experienced a very public and painful ruptured quad tendon during a church meeting in Portland, Oregon.

---

6. Jones and Wilson, *What's Next for Old First Church*, 8.
7. Jones and Wilson, *What's Next for Old First Church*, 8.

The first phase of the recovery was surgery, which repaired the injury and reattached the tendon. This needed to be completely straight and protected for several weeks. The second phase, which lasted several weeks, involved regaining the range of motion, bending the leg each day, from 30 degrees to 60 and then 90 and then 120 degrees. The third phase involved regaining strength in my leg; while the tendon was restored and flexibility was regained, the leg needed to become strong for walking and running to be possible!

I see this physical therapy as a metaphor for space. We can become rigid in our understanding of space, but with rigidity there is no movement or life! In recovery I had a real fear of pain, and this would often prevent me from stretching toward greater motion. And yet I wanted to regain the muscle memory that had allowed me to hike and play tennis; I wanted to walk my daughter down the aisle and dance with her at her wedding.

What is the muscle memory of a church's space? Can we move beyond a rigid preservation to a recovery of muscle memory—children playing, young people singing, adults laughing with joy? Can we imagine new forms of movement—the arts, dance, yoga, physical therapy? Can we regain the purposes of our buildings, to glorify their creator and to enhance community?

This will require adaptation, stretching, and at times some discomfort and pain! And yet this is a way to growth and strength as we lean into the missional purpose of our buildings.

Let Statistics Tell a Story

If you've gone to a doctor with an illness recently, you were probably disappointed if you left without a diagnosis. A doctor who simply says "You are sick" is the most frustrating kind of doctor. You might want to know the statistics surrounding your sickness. Is your blood pressure high? Do you have a fever? A knowledgeable doctor tells you exactly what is going on in your body. In the same way, the church's pastor and its leaders can't simply lean back and say "We are dying." Leaders can be more effective when letting statistics tell the story of a First Church. What statistics are helpful in measuring how "sick" a church is and how much time they "have left" varies in different contexts and regions, but important determining factors are the average age of worship attendees and the average age of financial-giving units. At the end of this chapter, you will find a worksheet to complete with your church leadership to help you understand your church's health through statistics.

"Old First Church" is a place and a property that holds pride in its long-standing relationships with major cities and towns across the US. In many ways the "Old First Church" speaks for the rest of us, because it had a privileged place and voice in the public square. The reality now is that "Old First Church" is fragile and only sustains that place as long as it honestly and rigorously is self-aware, finds ministry partners, and stays flexible. Old First Churches represent both the honor of our faith in the forming of our country as well as the horror of our faith in perpetuating, maintaining, and sometimes encouraging racist ideologies.

The complexities of running a museum are similar to that of simply trying to maintain "Old First Church." In these settings, leaders become not only preachers but property managers, interpreters, and plumbers to keep the legacy alive. We rent space while we wrestle with its implications. We follow Jesus to keep watch so that all are welcome and none are exploited. The moment to act for some "First Churches" is now. Many "First Churches" chose or will choose a slow death, which unfortunately silences the virtuous voice that "First Church" offers its city and country. If you are reading this book, you are reaching for the passion and desire to be a church for a city or town. This requires a church to look at its new neighbors and move back into the neighborhood.

Strategy Session

With your leadership group, ask the following questions:
Is your church an "Old First Church"? If not how is your church
similar to or different from the "Old First Church"?

What does it mean for churches to create spaces for different stake-
holders?

What is the role of a spiritual leader (lay or clergy) in interpreting
the meaning of these missional spaces within a ministry space or
sacred environment?

Your church statistics tell a story about the health of your church.
Take time with your leaders to fill out this worksheet and then explore what it might be telling you about your church and its health.

What is the average age of your worship attenders?	
What is the average age of your giving units?	
What percentage of your giving units are over the age of 65?	
How much revenue did you lose last year due to death of giving units?	
How much revenue did you lose last year due to people moving out of your city?	
How many new attenders did you gain last year?	
What is the average age of your new attenders?	
How many new giving units did you gain last year?	
What is the average age of your giving units?	
What percentage of your annual budget comes from tithes?	
What percentage of your annual budget comes from facility rentals?	
What percentage of your annual budget comes from your endowment?	
Over the next ten years what legacy gifts have been pledged that might come into fruition?	
In 20 years how many giving units do you expect will be still giving?	

Churches often live in their memories, and that prevents them from making decisions necessary to have a future tomorrow. Is your church in need of making a large change?

In what ways is your church working to stay ahead of the next wave?

Chapter 4

#MrRogersLife

As a child of the 1980s, I (Audrey) know by heart the tune to the educational program produced by Presbyterian pastor Mr. Rogers.[1] Do you know it or remember it? The lyrics are profound:

It's a beautiful day in the neighborhood,
a beautiful day for a neighbor.
Could you be mine?
Would you be mine?

It's a neighborly day in this beautywood,
a neighborly day for a beauty.
Would you be mine?
Could you be mine?

I have always wanted to have a neighbor just like you.
I've always wanted to live in a neighborhood with you.
So let's make the most of this beautiful day.
Since we're together, might as well say
would you be my, could you be my, won't you be my neighbor?

---

1. "Won't You Be My Neighbor?" written by Fred Rogers, © 1967, Fred M. Rogers. Used with permission.

Fred Rogers lived out Thomas Merton's experience of seeing everyone as "holy" and "shining like the sun." Mr. Rogers believed his neighborhood was beautiful and his neighbors were beautiful. He told his neighbors that he always wanted a neighbor just like them. For many church leaders this has been true—until your neighbors change! Single-family home dwellers or even apartment dwellers have the opportunity to move when the neighborhood changes. Some are even forced to move if the neighborhood changes. Churches are different. As a consequence, we get "drive-in" churches, where people who once lived near the church have moved far from the church and now "drive-in" to their church. There are fewer "drive-out" churches. This occurs when members move out far from the church and the church follows them, usually to the suburbs. It's possible that a denomination might plant a new church in a newly developed area or a stable church might begin a second campus closer to where members have moved, but most churches don't sell their current property and rebuild in a newly developed area to be closer to their members who have moved.

The consequences of a church staying in its property means that in an ever-changing society, its neighbors will probably change. For some this is a blessing and for others a curse, and for all it is a reality that we must embrace. We adapt to #mrrogerslife! For some rural churches, many neighbors have moved away, and they are now neighbor-less. For other rural churches, they have more neighbors than ever before because the pent-urban suburbs are creeping close to their small community. Downtown churches have neighbors who fluctuate between rich and poor, black and white, immigrants and military. Some have even found themselves in parts of town that have been renamed, such as Chinatown, Little Haiti, and Little Havana. In this chapter we give stories, scripture, and strategies that support us in the efforts to know our neighbor and our neighborhood, to live a #mrrogerslife.

Story 1-Wesley's Playhouse, England

In the heart of Birstall, England, is a church, Howden Clough Methodist Church. Like many churches, it had declined to an average worship attendance of six or seven people. The six or seven people were also aging and wondering how their church would move forward. When these people were younger in age, the town of Birstall was smaller. Slowly the neighborhood changed, and urban sprawl transformed the town into a thriving suburb of West Yorkshire, England. The church didn't know how to handle the shift and failed to reach out to young families with many distractions, such as regular soccer (football) games on Sundays.

In 2006, with only three thousand pounds in the bank, the church faced closure. They knew that if they wanted to stay alive, they would need to get to know their neighbors.

The church tried to engage their community in many ways. They first tried traditional forms of outreach, such as vacation Bible school and large events. Their efforts were in vain. The church began to get so desperate that they started going out into the community and asking their neighbors what they wanted and what they needed. They noticed that most families wanted and needed the same thing: a warm and safe place for their kids to play. One of the primary leaders was the trustees chair, Caroline Holt, who would later become a lay pastor. After listening to these desires, Caroline recalled her nephew's birthday party a few weeks prior. She celebrated her nephew at a Wacky Warehouse, an indoor playground. She began to ask the question, "What if we transformed our sanctuary into a giant playground?" Among the seven members, a couple scoffed at the idea and others thought it was brilliant. But they only had three thousand pounds in the bank.

Caroline wrote a few grant proposals and raised some funds from other Methodist organizations. One nonprofit gave 51,000 pounds to the project, and the church raised 30,000 pounds through other donors. Within eight months the newly renovated Sanctuary-Playground was blessed for business, and the newly named "Wesley Playhouse" opened its doors. Within the first few years, forty-two thousand people passed through its doors. It held a new weekly service for families, which averaged eighty in worship with eight baptisms within the first year. The church was earning money and could sustain itself into the future. In a short YouTube video on its work, Caroline says that any church can be transformed if it only lets go and looks forward.[2]

The story of the Wesley Playhouse points out that one of the primary purposes of the church is to get to know its neighbors. Once members knew their neighbors, and what they wanted and needed, they quickly began to dream about how they could connect using their resources and skills. The resource the church had was a building, a warm building with a high ceiling. Frederick Buechner says that our calling as Christians is "the place where [our] deep gladness and the world's deep hunger meet."[3] This was the case for this small church in England. Not only did it have space, it also had a few people with hearts to serve. The seven surviving church members became very involved in the Wesley Playhouse. Many members volunteered on a daily basis, making sandwiches to sell, baking cakes, and decorating for birthday parties.

The church "let go" of their building and embraced a new legacy for itself. The few members could have held on tightly to the past, but their church would have closed and would no longer be meeting. Their building might have continued to stand as a restaurant or bed and breakfast or community hall. This future ensued for many

2. Fresh Expressions, "The Wesley Playhouse," November 9, 2017, https://www.youtube.com/watch?v=BCMlrZHawXQ.

3. Frederick Buechner, *Wishful Thinking: A Theological ABC* (New York: Harper & Row, 1973).

church buildings in the UK and Europe. In reflecting upon this reality, Caroline says, "Perhaps our buildings will be the legacy of the lack of faith that some people have in actually stepping forward to see where people need the church, not the other way around."[4] Caroline's church placed the people and purpose of sharing the gospel above its love for their sanctuary and property. In turn, the church has kept its property and its purpose has transformed its members, it has added new members, and it has blessed its community. Their legacy is large! Our buildings have the opportunity to leave a powerful legacy, and so does our land.

Story 2—Dog Park in the Midwest

While land is hard to come by in big cities, it is plentiful in rural communities. Some churches not only have a building but also have a lot of land. Some bought the land hoping to expand, and others purchased many acres to one day have a cemetery. Still other churches receive large acres of land in wills and gifts. One church in the rural Midwest had a lot of land. Like other rural communities the town was becoming more of a bedroom community in a local suburb. The church is healthy and of medium size, with a proven desire to bring new people into a relationship with Christ, and with new friends. The pastor of the church is an innovator and entrepreneur and often wondered what could be done with all their land. The answer came through his own wife who told him what she and others needed.

Most Sundays after Don returned home from morning worship, his wife would head out the door with their dog. One week, he saw her packing up to leave and noticed she had a bunch of cupcakes. He learned the cupcakes were not for him, but for dogs and puppy parents. Each Sunday his wife headed out to a dog park in the next

---

4. Fresh Expressions, "The Wesley Playhouse."

township over, which was about twenty minutes away. That specific day one of the dogs had a birthday, and she signed up to bring cupcakes. Don learned that his wife was part of this interesting dog community. The dog group met weekly, cared for one another, ate with one another, and did a lot of things a church would do.

Don went to his church leadership with the idea of creating a dog park on its land. The church members had mixed emotions, but it didn't matter how they felt, because they didn't have money for it. Don offered to write grant proposals. He made a deal with the church that if he could find the money, it would provide the land. Within one month Don had a large grant from the city to pay for the entire dog park, *and* the city would maintain the park. The church made good on its part of the deal and allocated the land to the city through a land lease. The dog park is now a gathering place for their community. The church holds services at the park and hosts an annual dog park festival that draws over a hundred and twenty thousand people each year. The church "let go" of some land and in turn has earned a lot more money than the land is worth through their festivals, which fund the mission of the church. Learning what its neighbors needed was the key to the property project. In many ways the people guided what happened on the property. What is healthy for our community and our neighbors is healthy for our church. Our health is intertwined with that of the people who live around us.

Scripture

Scripture is clear on being a good neighbor and defining who that might be. This possibly explains why a pastor formed by scripture created a show focused on the neighborhood. The Shema is one of the central prayers in the Hebrew Bible. It is located in Deuteronomy 6:5 and reads: "Love the LORD your God with all your heart, all your being, and all your strength." Jesus quotes the Shema in the New Testament when questioned by a lawyer about how to inherit eternal life. Jesus expanded this rule for life with a commandment from Leviticus 19:18, by saying it like this, "You must love the Lord your God with all your heart, with all your being, and with all your mind . . . [and] love your neighbor as yourself" (Matthew 22:37, 39). *Our salvation is bound up with our relationship to our neighbor. The salvation of our church community is also bound up with our relationships with our neighbors.*

Some churches might ask a clarifying question much like the lawyer did, "Who exactly is my neighbor?" Drive-in churches might ask, "Who is my neighbor? The people who live around me or the people who live around the church?" Jesus responded to the lawyer with a story about the good Samaritan. Martin Luther King Jr. focused on this text in his last address before he was assassinated. In his sermon he ponders why the Levite and the priest passed by without helping. Perhaps the Samaritan was avoided for the sake of cleansing rituals that qualify a worshipper to enter the temple courts. Perhaps the priest was on his way to an important temple meeting. Use your imagination, like the preacher did, as he compared the two possible questions the Levite and the good Samaritan might have asked. He imagined that the Levite's first question was, "'If I stop to help this man, what will happen to me?" He then imagined that the good Samaritan reversed the question asking, "If I do not stop to help this man, what will happen to him?"[5]

In the questions asked by the three sojourners we understand that our actions produce reactions and are caught up in circumstances of the people around us. In addition, if you take the question of the Levite and the priest and replace it with the question asked by

---

5. Martin Luther King Jr., "I've Been to the Mountain Top," last sermon delivered at Mason Temple (Church of God in Christ Headquarters), Memphis, TN, April 3, 1968.

the lawyer directly after Jesus expands the Shema, one might receive an affirming answer, "You will receive eternal life." The Levite and the priest were not thinking about the kingdom when they passed by; instead, they were thinking of themselves. When practicing the Christian faith, we absolutely must give up thinking only of ourselves. Our salvation is caught up in the salvation of the other.

A particular king in the New Testament learned this the hard way. In the story of the rich ruler and Lazarus, Luke tells it best:

> There was a certain rich man who clothed himself in purple and fine linen, and who feasted luxuriously every day. At his gate lay a certain poor man named Lazarus who was covered with sores. Lazarus longed to eat the crumbs that fell from the rich man's table. Instead, dogs would come and lick his sores. The poor man died and was carried by angels to Abraham's side.
>
> The rich man also died and was buried. While being tormented in the place of the dead, he looked up and saw Abraham at a distance with Lazarus at his side. He shouted, "Father Abraham, have mercy on me. Send Lazarus to dip the tip of his finger in water and cool my tongue, because I'm suffering in this flame."
>
> But Abraham said, "Child, remember that during your lifetime you received good things, whereas Lazarus received terrible things. Now Lazarus is being comforted and you are in great pain. Moreover, a great crevasse has been fixed between us and you. Those who wish to cross over from here to you cannot. Neither can anyone cross from there to us."
>
> The rich man said, "Then I beg you, Father, send Lazarus to my father's house. I have five brothers. He needs to warn them so that they don't come to this place of agony."
>
> Abraham replied, "They have Moses and the Prophets. They must listen to them."
>
> The rich man said, "No, Father Abraham! But if someone from the dead goes to them, they will change their hearts and lives."
>
> Abraham said, "If they don't listen to Moses and the Prophets, then neither will they be persuaded if someone rises from the dead."
> (Luke 16:19-31 CEB)

The rich ruler doesn't have a name. Often in a parable the story-teller implies that we should place our own name in the place of the nameless character. Luke tells us that the rich man has a neighbor and his name is Lazarus. The rich man's inability to see him as his neighbor was a problem and quite possibly landed him in hell. In heaven the rich man reached out to Lazarus. Instead of asking for a cup of sugar or glass of milk, he desperately asks Father Abraham, who was next to Lazarus, for a drop of cool water for his tongue. The rich man needed Lazarus in the afterlife, but he ignored and did not understand Lazarus's need for him in earthly life.

One way to interpret this parable is to presume the theological role reversal in the afterlife, and conclude that Jesus has a preferential option for the poor. This point of view is helpful in some teaching. Consider also that this parable shows how complex our lives and relationships are on earth, because our relationships here and now are bound up with our salvation now and always. Eternity begins before death on earth inasmuch we are able to see heaven on earth by seeing and treating each human being as our neighbor.

Strategy—Go to Your Neighbors

So how do we get to know our neighbor? How do we move back into our neighborhood? Recently, I (Audrey) moved out of a parsonage and into an apartment building downtown. I lived there for a year while the church parsonage was renovated. Before I moved downtown, I knew a few of my neighbors but not many. As I contemplated moving back into my neighborhood, I wondered how I might get to know more of my neighbors. I imagined hosting a big party for my neighbors, asking them to come to me. I still hope to do this because I love parties, and I intend to promote our contractors and their business. However, I find so far that I get to know my neighbors best by going to them, by walking my dog around my neighborhood. Similarly, in the church, we often hope our neighbors will come to us. We think that if we plan a great party or VBS or rummage sale, that our neighbors will come by and want to be one of us. In some communities this might work, but in our rapidly changing and diversifying culture, people are not coming into churches. People must be met along the road.

A sociology professor from Wofford College spent a year exploring the power of one's neighborhood. For an entire year he spent all his time in a two-mile radius of his home. He found that his health improved in that year, physically and emotionally. He felt more connected and whole. He felt like he belonged somewhere and to somebody. The same is possible for our churches. As we learned from the stories earlier in this chapter, churches became healthier when they focused on the people directly around them and when they went to them. A strategy to help us live a #mrrogerslife is to go to our neighbor. The neighbors living right around our block, in a two-mile radius. Getting to know our neighbors is one of the keys in learning how to build and rebuild our churches, inside and out.

Strategy—Build from the Outside In

For years, in the practice of architecture, creative designers placed the form of a building over the function of the building. The process began with a pretty picture and then solved the space for how the people would move about it. This philosophy still works for some projects. However, when trying to build a space for everyone, the people and purpose of a building drives what is ultimately created, and the form follows. Millennial lifestyles and values have, in part, led to this shift away from traditional design.

In many ways, the economic movement of millennials can be seen as a venture into virtue. Some blame this venture to virtue on the technological revolution and believe that millennials are so tied to their screens that they need nothing else. The religious right does not believe it is a religiously inspired move, and they might even say the lifestyle is not a venture back to virtue. Economists, by and large, blame the US recession of 2008. I blame the rise of a Swedish furniture store that specializes in small spaces: Ikea!

Economists may be right. The birth of tiny and communal living emerges as much out of necessity as it does from desire. In 2008 and the difficult years following, many millennials watched their parents move or moved with them when they lost their house during the real-estate foreclosures in the United States. This loss created a fear of buying a house for many millennials. One might wonder if the sudden loss of home or dramatic change in lifestyle might cause an entire generation to hold lightly their possessions and rather invest their time and money in experiences and community.[6]

In addition to the risk factor of purchasing a home, many millennials simply cannot afford to do so. In 2013, *USA Today* reported, "With a median household income of $40,581, millennials earn 20 percent less than boomers did at the same stage of life, despite being better educated, according to a new analysis of Federal Reserve data by the advocacy group Young Invincibles."[7] Not only are millennials earning less, they also have massive tuition debts to pay off, and their overall net worth is less than their parents' was at their age. "The median net worth of millennials is $10,090, 56 percent less than it

---

6. Anna Bahney, "How the Financial Crisis Affected Millennials, 10 Years Later," *CNN Money*, December 4, 2017, https://money.cnn.com/2017/12/04/pf/impact-recession-millennials/index.html.

7. Collin Brennan, "Millennials Earn 20 % Less Than Boomers Did at the Same Stage of Life," *USA TODAY*, January 13, 2017, https://www.usatoday.com/story/money/2017/01/13/millennials-falling-behind-boomer-parents/96530338/.

was for boomers."[8] The Progressive Policy Institute reports that even since the year 2000 real earnings for college grads have gone down by 10 percent. Most millennials realize that they will have a lower standard of living than their parents.[9]

Whether the movement toward virtue is caused by technology, religion, or economics, it is one that leaders in the Christian faith can address. The concept of sharing is one remedy leveraged by millennial start-ups. The movement away from home ownership and car ownership (which requires mass transit in walkable cities) sounds consistent with Acts 2 and 4, with earliest Christians holding property in common.

One Miami developer, Ryan Shear, with Property Markets Group listened to his neighbors (the young people living around him) and studied the data of this group. The values of young adults in Miami and elsewhere birthed the micro-unit movement in Miami. The needs and values of the target group and their neighborhood would determine how the building was built and what happened inside. The goal was to give millennials an attainable price point to live downtown. This was the starting point. In further listening to millennials they learned that apartment size was not a large value, but community space was important to them. The building then became built around the philosophy of smaller personal spaces and large public spaces. The communal areas included a pool deck as big as a cruise ship, large grills to cook out, a theater to watch big games or season finales, a large open-to-the-public bar and coffee shop in the lobby, and a gym equipped for personal use and group classes. The function of the desired user determined the form the building would

8. "Millennials Earn 20% Less than Boomers Did at the Same Stage of Life."
9. J. Maureen Henderson, "Millennials Earn Less Than Their Parents and the Recession Isn't to Blame," *Forbes*, November 30, 2013, https://www.forbes.com /sites/jmaureenhenderson/2013/11/30/millennials-earn-less-than-their-parents -and-the-recession-isnt-to-blame/#773a83f45946.

take both inside and out. Due to the large spaces in size and the overall budget for the project, there is no large glass curtain around the building or a noticeable architectural feature that makes it stand out. Instead, choosing to stay within the budget and reflect its users' value on art, the building has large multistory pieces of art that are printed on vinyl. The art can be seen from blocks away. The developer designed from the outside in by (1) looking first to those in the neighborhood and who would be moving to the neighborhood, (2) listening to who they are and what they value, and (3) building a product that they could both financially and socially "buy into."

How might the church think about its current space, future space, programs, and mission with this outside-in thinking? What might our neighbors teach us about how to create more inviting and inclusive spaces? What new people might venture into spaces if built just for them? As if the church had been waiting for a neighbor just like them?

Strategy—Let Go and Let God!

"Let Go and Let God" is a familiar cliché Christians have told one another for decades. We've worn the bracelet and really tried emotionally to let go of things. This strategy is not so much about emotionally "letting go" but actually, physically "letting go" of stuff. At times it's difficult for a church, pastor, and even developer to "let go" of old ideas for how things should be done, so that they embrace the next life ahead. Consider the story of a church with a sanctuary as well as ten classrooms. Not one classroom was used for ministry; instead the rooms were used for storage. The neighborhood around the church had changed. Over the course of a decade, the new neighbors around the church primarily spoke Spanish and were from a different culture with different traditions than most members. One day a member of the community went to the pastor and said, "Your parking lot seems to be empty during the week. I run a school for autistic children, and we are currently looking for a new place to meet. Could we begin a conversation?"

The pastor and church soon began a conversation with him. The church realized they had to "let go" in order to let God do a new thing. They physically had to let go of their stuff in order to make space for this new group to come in. The church made an amazing shift. The church also started a monthly worship service for the family and friends of the students , who could not attend Sunday mornings because they had to work. That service sometimes had twice as many congregants present as the service on Sunday mornings. The church had to let go of some worship patterns to make room for their neighbors with new needs.

Our neighbors, the neighbors living directly around our church, have changed. No matter where you live, this is probably true. As new waves of immigrants and as new generations of our children spread across the land, our culture and our nation has resisted these changes. Some churches and neighborhoods expect people to become like them and to speak like them if allowed in the neighborhood. In welcoming our new neighbors, in getting to know them, in seeing them as beautiful and the neighborhood as beautiful, we become the leaders Christ calls us to be. We become a bit more like Mr. Rogers and a lot more like Jesus. Jesus came to us, became like us, and moved into our neighborhood. The third-century theologian Athanasius stated, "God became man so that man might become God."[10]

Even Paul tells the readers of Corinthians to do whatever it takes to know those around you and work towards their salvation and your own.

---

10. Athanasius, "Section 54," in *On the Incarnation*, trans. John Behr (Yonkers, NY: St. Vladimir's Seminary Press, 2012).

Although I'm free from all people, I make myself a slave to all people, to recruit more of them. I act like a Jew to the Jews, so I can recruit Jews. I act like I'm under the Law to those under the Law, so I can recruit those who are under the Law (though I myself am not under the Law). I act like I'm outside the Law to those who are outside the Law, so I can recruit those outside the Law (though I'm not outside the law of God but rather under the law of Christ). I act weak to the weak, so I can recruit the weak. I have become all things to all people, so I could save some by all possible means. All the things I do are for the sake of the gospel, so I can be a partner with it. (1 Cor 9:19-23 CEB)

Paul understood that sharing in the blessings means sharing the gospel with his neighbors, not restricting the good news to those already in the temple.

Strategy Session

Gather a group of people from your church and answer the following questions:

You have permission to draw in this book. Think about the neighborhood around your church. On the next pages, draw a picture of your neighborhood, illustrating roughly a two-mile radius around your church.

Compare your diagram or image with others in your group. What is similar and what is different?

On your smartphone, go to your "maps" app and type in the address of your church. Zoom in and then take some time looking at the features around your church. Compare your maps, which were hand-drawn, to the map in your smart-phone app. Whose map includes most of the items found on your map app?

Brainstorm with your group about how you might engage one of the neighbors around your church. What is the name of this person, organization or business?

Chapter 5

#RealLife

The Real World from MTV was the first reality show on television. The show was about handfuls of twenty-something young adults who moved together into a gorgeous house in California. Cameras were present and would often follow them around. The show depicted the group dealing with what life was like in the "real world" and navigating that with other people. The group learned how to make decisions together, cook together, and eat together. Life happened with a lot of drama, tears, fighting, and a few romantic encounters. Teens and young adults were hooked on the show after a few minutes of watching.

In retrospect, it is ridiculous to think that the show portrayed "real life." For anyone else, real life is not living in a gorgeous house in California with your bills paid and then getting paid for being on camera. Although the show's financial construct required suspending disbelief, the issues dealt with on the show were real in the 1990s. The show tackled race, HIV/AIDS, sex, prejudice, death, politics, and substance abuse. The small group of participants helped the rest of the world understand the realities at play around the world. They learned how to be "adult" without killing one another and learned what it means to truly love one another even in the midst of conflict.

Some reality shows depict real life, and other series seem to depict real life within a bubble. This variation also applies to churches. Some faith communities depict real life, and some live in a church bubble. A church bubble is usually experienced when we believe we can keep on living or behaving or making decisions without knowledge or understanding of the real world around us. Churches continue to function in this way until a reality check comes, often on payday when the church treasurer cannot pay the staff and the bank account reads "insufficient funds."

For some reason in real life, effective financial and business leaders are able to make hard decisions, create strategic plans, and take risks. Yet with the work-avoidance of the church, many of us take off our business hats. In the effort to "live out the gospel" or do ministry apart from worldly principles, our churches end up in a financial crisis and with the same vision statement and logo developed thirty years in the past. Preachers are fond of the saying "be in the world, but not of the world." This phrase is not found in scripture.

Jesus, Paul, and other apostles encourage us to keep our eyes on the kingdom of heaven, which is here in many ways and not yet here in other ways. We are often reminded through stories in scripture that there is more reality than we can see in this world. So, we say with the Lord's Prayer, "they kingdom come, on earth as it is in heaven." The kingdom of heaven is here now, brought incarnate to this earth, and whether we like it or not, we live in this real world.

To survive and thrive in the real world, we will also need partners. More and more churches need collaborators and helpers to carry out their mission. How does a church do this faithfully and legally? In this chapter we dive into stories, scripture, and strategies that help us live faithfully in relationship with the real world. We look at ways in which churches have expanded their data sources to figure out how to best use their space. We also share models for how churches forge relationships with one another and community nonprofits to open up a revenue stream and refuel their mission.

Story—Church, Schools, and Taxes

Have you noticed a church with bars on its front doors? I (Audrey) have encountered quite a few in Miami. At first glance, one might assume the church is condemned or permanently closed, but after you consider the context, the bars on the doors simply mean "we are not open right now." This was partially true for a church I encountered in Miami. Bars were on the front doors to keep people from coming inside. On Sunday, members slipped around the back door. This church had been in decline for some time. A school met at the church, but it was very disconnected from the church culture and the office of the pastor. On some days the church was without a pastor. The few people who attended kept up their historic building and prayer through the income from the school and occasional renting of the parking lot.

In 2010 a new pastor arrived, and his mission made people his top priority. He started with the school. The pastor and his spouse befriended teachers and worked with the school to hire new staff and create a new culture there. Small improvements were made to the property—taking the bars off the doors—and included new safety and security features. The majority of the pastor's time, though, was spent on the people around the church. The school began to grow, and with the growth other renovations and upgrades happened on the property. A new relevant worship service was created, and soon enough the church saw a turnaround in worship. Over a period of five years, the seemingly abandoned church became a church in and for and with the city around it. The church is not a megachurch (few in Miami are mega), and it averaged a few hundred people in worship as it listened to the people around it and became part of the neighborhood.

The key relationship that continued to bring new life and revenue to the church was the school. This reality only occurred inasmuch as the church brought life and love to the school. The relationship was symbiotic, with each organization helping the other and causing each other to rise. Another key relationship developed with food trucks in the area. The church soon opened its parking lot to food trucks that could set up in a spot next to the church. In making the parking deal with the food trucks, the pastor arranged for staff at the church and school to receive a meal card, where they could eat free at the food trucks. Through these vital and revenue-producing relationships, the church found its footing again.

All were happy with this growth, and still are, but along the way they encountered a snafu. Taxes! The church and pastor were not aware that the school meeting at the church for over seven years was a for-profit entity. Perhaps some church people were aware, but their thinking was contained in a church bubble. The food trucks also posed a problem, since they too did not qualify as nonprofit ventures. The school and the mobile eateries were making money on church property, which went untaxed. The church's relationships went unnoticed until the county property appraiser caught on. Soon the front page of the local newspaper reported that there was a seven-million-dollar lien placed on the property to make up for past property taxes.

The church and its lawyers are still negotiating (as of the publication date of this book) with the city. The church will be okay since it has property assets, such as its parking lot, that it could sell if needed to cover the bill. The church will pay something. We might think it was worth the risk, though the church didn't realize it was taking a risk. A property fine that a church can eventually pay is worth the growth and new life and new disciples the church has created.

Skeptics might shame and scold the leaders for not knowing. However, the leaders did the best they could with a turnaround at the time. The church had been in transition from leaders moving and pastors coming and going. No wonder financial details and arrangements got lost. But, at the end of the day, the best-case scenario would have occurred if the church had known how to enter into the agreements properly, so that the required taxes would have been paid. In the real world, the church needs revenue streams to continue its mission. This is also true for Habitat for Humanity, Big Brothers Big Sisters, Young Life, and many other nonprofits trying to make a Jesus difference in the lives of people.

Story—Models of Relationships

The paradigm for growth in ministry is often dependent on planting churches. The regional governing office of the denomination would identify a growing area. A parsonage would be purchased for the pastor who would go to the community to build a church. Funds would be given to help the pastor learn the community, identify leaders, and eventually launch a worship service or adult small groups in a local school gym or cafeteria. Eventually the church would grow to over 150 people in worship, purchase land, and begin a capital campaign. Once the funds were raised to the standard of the loan agreement, the church would start to build its permanent sanctuary and other buildings. The church would then go on maintaining its building and mission through tithes and fundraisers.

In most denominations and even among independent pioneers this method appeared to work for a long time—though the judicatory data shows that the success rate has always been low. Most new church starts don't last past their founding pastor, and few ever move out of the school gym. Most know that forty-year-old buildings are hard to maintain, but most new church starts won't get to the point of breaking ground. Due to the low success rate, we are always looking for new approaches and alternatives to planting new congregations.

This chapter documents stories of how there are fresh ways for existing churches with property to take risks rather than close. We often have more options than we realize. An existing congregation, however small, can partner with someone else, and thus continue to share the gospel. The stories of these partnerships are arranged into three categories or themes: (1) the renter (2) the roommate (3) the redevelopment.

The Renter

In South Florida (and across the thirty largest US cities) the cost of property and maintenance is astronomical. Building is expensive, maintaining paint affected by salty air is expensive, and insurance is expensive. Not only is a facility expensive financially but it also eats away at the time of our pastors and laypeople to do the ministry of teaching, preaching, worship, pastoral care, and outreach. For this reason, many new church starts develop their ministry as renters. Examples of this approach are Miami Vineyard (http://www.miamivineyard.com) and Vous Church (https://www.vouschurch.com). Both churches are nondenominational. They don't have a large pot of new-church-development money for a safety net if they have a few hard months or can't quite meet a mortgage for a few months. In some ways, moving into a permanent space seems to prove riskier than living together with a variable (rather than fixed) cost as renters. Two types of renter fit this pattern.

The "continuous renter" arrangement suggests that a church will rent space that it can use all the time. Churches rent spaces such as a large warehouse to achieve this goal. The church doesn't own the space but rents it, and it is adapted to its specifications. In many cases, the church will rent a large space and then build out the space as it needs it. The space is still stable to meet its needs, but it does not have the large overhead cost of maintenance for the building or air conditioning unit. Church leaders in old buildings shudder when they hear the words *air conditioning unit* or *heater*. These large machines are often the sole reason for many closed churches. In the variable cost, "continuous renter" model, the church doesn't need to worry about unexpected system failures in the building. It has a negotiated rental rate, with no surprises. And if the building is not maintained by the owner, it can end the lease and locate to another building.

With the "pop-up rental" model, a church makes the decision to rent space for a certain number of hours each week, pops up as a church during those hours, and then pops out. Now imagine a traditional new-church start that opts to function this way indefinitely. It seems exhausting, but it is done and with great success in some places. In Naples, Florida, one of the fastest growing churches is called Celebration Beach Church (https://celebrationbeachchurch .com). At this church you can worship and get a tan at the same time. This is my (Audrey's) sort of church. The church meets every week in a park close to the beach. It invites guests to wear flip-flops and bring their pets. They have coffee, fellowship, sermon series, an offering, a band, baptisms, and all the wonderful things a permanent church structure has, except it rents the park space. Celebration Beach Church pops up in the park and then pops out. The church averages over 250 people each week. Their overhead costs are low and manageable for a church starting out. Pop-up churches may have office space and storage space, but those spaces are small and usually rented as well.

The Roommate

The "roommate" model is operating when a church with property rents its space to an outside group or another church. Or the church simply gives space to an outside group or another church.

Each individual church must weigh the financial needs and mission of the church to understand what it can offer to a group. In this model the church gains a roommate. Most of us have had roommates and know the complexities of the relationship. The roommate model for churches requires carefully-thought about relationships. Churches invite numerous types of roommates to live with them, including other churches, afterschool programs, private schools, nonprofits, and self-help programs. Like the renter model, there are two types of roommates, continuous roommates and pop-up roommates.

Continuous roommates should establish a relationship with mutual understanding, and if possible stipulate the features, benefits, and boundaries in a legal agreement, which helps the two entities to remain roommates into the future. Branches United Methodist Church has a permanent roommate called Branches Inc., an afterschool program. The story of these roommates is found in chapter 1 of this book. In short, the missional church could not survive on its own. Its property was the resource to leverage. The annual conference for the denomination, through a trust clause, legally owns the land, so it entered into a fifty-year lease agreement (two twenty-five year renewals) with Branches Inc. The two entities are very clear that they are in a "covenant relationship" and not merely living together for a hundred years. In this covenant, both roommates have space that is their own and some that is shared. Each group has permanent signage and mailboxes. This "continuous renter" model works better when the mission of both entities is clear and similar. There will always be conflict to resolve, but the larger mission and vision keeps the two groups together. In best-case scenarios, both "roomies" are clear that they need each other.

The "pop-up roommate" is a short-term arrangement that might last for a few years, and is typically based on a legal agreement renewed on a year-to-year basis. Some churches have dedicated rooms they use for the pop-up roommate. They live together throughout the whole week, but their mission and purpose might be altogether different. This model is helpful to a church financially. This model might be easier for some churches to maintain, since they might not have the time or infrastructure to properly engage their roommates. The pop-up roommate can also generate traffic on-site and bring people into the actual church building who otherwise might never otherwise do so. The pop-up roommate relationship means that the church can maintain its own identity while still opening its doors to other groups. The church has a permanent sign and the pop-up roommate often communicates its presence by movable banners.

The Redevelopment

Redevelopment is more extreme than renting or rooming, because a church leverages its entire building to create something new. Churches in large cities with great property value lead the way with this model. The redevelopment model often includes selling property, leasing land, and transforming or completely rebuilding the church building into something new. In cities where property is very scarce, such as New York City and Washington, DC a land lease is attractive. A church can lease its land to a developer for fifty or more years. The developer will develop the land. The church can choose whether to use part of its lease income to build a new facility on the property or elsewhere. The church can choose to keep a large amount of money in an endowment for a continual revenue stream.

The redevelopment model also applies to churches and administrative offices that sell their land completely. They too may decide to stay onsite or move elsewhere. They will decide if they want to keep some money to invest in an endowment, fully fund a pension fund or scholarship, or spend it all in building a new property. Cities with more available land for development might choose this approach, since it is what the market allows and also provides for them the highest purchase price. Cities like Miami, Nashville, and Los Angeles include churches redeveloping in this way.

The redevelopment model does not generally stimulate an instant turnaround. Some of the more effective redevelopment models occur when a church chooses to either close or merge with another church, or both.

- In southern Miami (Dade County), two churches only a few miles apart made this courageous decision. They both officially closed and reopened under a new name. They sold one property and used the proceeds to fund the renovation of their other property while maintaining some funds in their endowment. They are on a long journey to new life, which takes confidence and hard work, because sometimes a merger doesn't reverse the inevitable outcome in a changing neighborhood.

- Other churches have closed and given themselves to another church. Church of the Resurrection near Kansas City and The Gathering (https://gatheringnow.org) near St. Louis worked with churches that were about to close in order to create a new satellite congregation in a changing zip code.

- Home Church (https://www.homechurchnashville.com) is a church restart in the space where Inglewood United Methodist Church met for many decades.

- Grace Church in Ft. Myers, FL (http://www.egracechurch .com) repurposes property to host dinner churches and gradually bring a church to a new beginning. Churches who choose to either close or merge internally with their denomination or both, can often redevelop their spaces into something new.

Each approach—renter, roommate, and redevelopment—overlaps in some characteristics, and in some places it is possible to combine all three approaches. For example, Branches United Methodist Church is a hybrid of a redevelopment model and a roommate model. They redeveloped the property through a land lease agreement, and as part of that agreement they would be roommates with Branches Inc. While pursuing a redevelopment approach, a church is often pushed into renting during its transition, while waiting for its new facilities to be built. Healthy churches are exploring and experimenting with different approaches to create new revenue streams and relationships, which work toward their clarified mission. Many pastors don't like to talk about money, and most church participants prefer not to hear about it. Some pastors even boast about mentioning money once a year from the pulpit. One way to get out of the denial that persists inside a "church bubble" is to talk about real life, which includes personal and church finance. Jesus himself spent more time talking about money than any other part of real life.

Scripture

The book of Matthew shares an insightful parable about stewardship. In the parable of the talents, Jesus encourages his listeners to stop being lazy and take a risk.

"The kingdom of heaven is like a man who was leaving on a trip. He called his servants and handed his possessions over to them. To one he gave five valuable coins, and to another he gave two, and to another he gave one. He gave to each servant according to that servant's ability. Then he left on his journey.

"After the man left, the servant who had five valuable coins took them and went to work doing business with them. He gained five more. In the same way, the one who had two valuable coins gained two more. But the servant who had received the one valuable coin dug a hole in the ground and buried his master's money.

"Now after a long time the master of those servants returned and settled accounts with them. The one who had received five valuable coins came forward with five additional coins. He said, 'Master, you gave me five valuable coins. Look, I've gained five more.'

"His master replied, 'Excellent! You are a good and faithful servant! You've been faithful over a little. I'll put you in charge of much. Come, celebrate with me.'

"The second servant also came forward and said, 'Master, you gave me two valuable coins. Look, I've gained two more.'

"His master replied, 'Well done! You are a good and faithful servant. You've been faithful over a little. I'll put you in charge of much. Come, celebrate with me.'

"Now the one who had received one valuable coin came and said, 'Master, I knew that you are a hard man. You harvest grain where you haven't sown. You gather crops where you haven't spread seed. So I was afraid. And I hid my valuable coin in the ground. Here, you have what's yours.'

"His master replied, 'You evil and lazy servant! You knew that I harvest grain where I haven't sown and that I gather crops where I haven't spread seed? In that case, you should have turned my money over to the bankers so that when I returned, you could give me what belonged to me with interest.'" (Matt 25:14-27 CEB)

The parable imagines three ways to steward the resources we are given. The first servant who was given five talents took them and somehow multiplied them. He used his resource as an investment resource. He invested in someone or something else and helped it flourish, and in turn it helped him flourish. The second servant did likewise. He was given two talents and came back with four, doubling his funds. The last servant was given one talent. He was afraid. His fear caused him to simply bury his talent and gain no more than he was given. He maintained his one talent but did not grow.

In the parable's teaching we understand that Jesus values faith over fear. The motivation to guard and hide was driven by fear. In our church settings fear is often the motivation controlling our financial situations. We want to freeze, preserve, and simply maintain what we have been given. Our fear paralyzes us from stepping forward and working out how our resources might lead to new relationships and revenue streams. Risk does not produce reward overnight, especially where risk-taking is neither impulsive nor presumed to happen by chance. Risk exposes our insecurities, but it generates imagination and is inspiring the good news that lead to renewal and revival in our church and community.

Strategy

Risk Wisely

One favorite parable involves the sower. A farmer goes out and sows some seeds. The parable speaks of the farmer sowing on rocky soil, weedy soil, and good soil. It does not require farm experience to know that the seeds grew when sowed into the good soil. Another implication from the parable is that a farmer "wasted" seeds by sowing them into every type of soil. My friend Roy Terry refers to the story as "The Parable of the Foolish Farmer." In the parable we are invited to sow our seeds, without consideration for whether the seeds will grow. I (Audrey) have used this reading of the parable in sermons and youth talks, by encouraging each person to invest in everyone and not overlook anyone. You might waste the effort, but that is okay, because the effort is for the kingdom of God.

This kind of risk-taking described in the parable rings true for sharing the good news, but it would be foolish to apply the parable to property and finance. We must risk our resources, but we should do so wisely.

Financial analysts are obviously aware of what drives risk, especially with market forces, yet they depend heavily on principles discerned by sociologists and psychologists. Adam Grant teaches at Wharton and wrote *Originals: How Non-Conformists Move the World.* He dives deep into how entrepreneurs and risk takers think and what makes them successful. For example, a group of young men ask him to invest in their eyeglasses start-up. Grant asked many questions and finally decided not to fund them, because it did not seem like they were "all in." Two of the guys still had other jobs, and only one of them was actually working full-time on the start-up. A few years later Grant regretted his decision. The company, Warby Parker, is thriving and is realizing its mission of providing people affordable glasses. Grant dove into entrepreneurial research and realized that many entrepreneurs, including Bill Gates and Mark Zuckerberg, did not give up everything to start their businesses, though they both dropped out of Harvard to start a business. Each founder, in his own way, mitigated his risk with another job or a plan to finish his undergraduate degree. They took a risk, but they each had a plan. *Although their risks were driven by passion and mission they were supported by math and maturity.*

In our own way, the entrepreneurial church leaders are called to take great risks and to plan wisely with intelligent advice, and measurable data. Making a good decision and understanding *why* we made the decision are important for the church's health and survival. We manage risk on a learning curve. For example, in the Western North Carolina and North Carolina conferences, the leadership relies on a partnership with the Duke Endowment, which funds research and gathers data concerning local church properties. This research reveals a few realities about church property.

Expert professional experience, which is in many churches available within the membership, is very important to decision-making church property. Two experts in property and finance contribute advice to this chapter and share wisdom about general business practices and finance.

Business Is a Blessing[1]

The words *church* and *business* often don't mix well. Some of the discomfort comes from stories and conflicts throughout church history. In many places the church became inseparable from the state and owned as much as one-third of all the land in a European nation or city. Given the potential for money to corrupt, it can be hard to reconcile business and ministry and understand the importance of each to the other. The church has much to teach the business world, and the business world has a few tips that sustain the church.

Be humble. We don't know what we don't know. Throughout the process of reimagining a future for our First Church in Miami, we constantly reminded ourselves that there was much we did not know. At our table we had accountants, lawyers, business professionals, doctors, bankers, and developers. Still there were many things we did not know. With church property assume that you know nothing. Hire help when needed. Some people are generous and donate their time to the church or offer their services on a retainer agreement. In our case, lawyers and accountants waived their fees until our property deal finally went through. Their expertise helped us tremendously.

Remember relationships. Business is always about relationships; so is ministry. After the project is complete, you will probably see each business or group you work with again. Be kind and respectful. In all your encounters remember that you represent the congregation and

---

1. Author's personal communication with Jason Randolph, trustees chair, First United Methodist Church, Miami.

God's mission to transform the world. Remind your partners that business is about relationships. Before engaging a firm, a nonprofit, or other organization, be sure to know how they can financially give to your church and be a partner with your mission. This strategy helped us work with all firms that we had interviewed—even the firms that we did not choose to work on our redevelopment project.

Keep the long view. In making business decisions it is easy to make a quick decision for your current needs. Throughout our project, to inform decisions, we keep in mind our ten-year plan. We often ask "what if" and guard ourselves from unnecessary risk. We constantly balance what is needed now and what can wait. We cannot have everything all at once; "scope creep" creates unnecessary risk. Like the Israelites we remember that the promised land is around the corner while we work through any momentary conflicts with patience and purpose.

Conflict is inherent to change. If you aren't comfortable with internal and external conflict, let someone else do the work. Being kind and humble doesn't eliminate conflict. Kindness is one way to work through conflict, but it does not negate it. Get comfortable with conflict and turn toward each other and not away from each other.

Finances That Foster a Future[2]

The finance committee of a church is a team that many avoid. Yet the finance committee also has the means to foster and guide church finances in a way that helps secure a future for the church and the gospel. The following financial tips emerged from the experience of chairing a financial committee in a church. Notice the themes of trust and clear communication.

---

2.   Author's personal communication with Ed Deppman, chair, finance committee, First United Methodist Church of Miami.

To maintain the congregation's trust in any financial decision, leaders and interested parties need an understanding of the bylaws and articles of incorporation. These documents ensure that decision-makers have been granted the responsibility to make those decisions. This trust also applies to a process as basic as bookkeeping: who is ultimately responsible for your church's transactions?

Accounting software (or for small or micro-churches, spreadsheets or paper diaries) should be selected to meet the specific needs by size of a church, its polity, and its clergy. Church management means tracking traditional and modern family relationships, spiritual gifts, congregant talents and interests, attendance, nursery security, contribution/fundraising campaigns, volunteer assignments, and small groups. For the medium and large churches, these metrics go beyond what is offered by software systems designed for commercial business. Investing in accounting/management systems may be expensive and involve an upfront investment in time and effort, but it will pay dividends in the future.

Written accounting policies covering all sources of funds and distributions will provide guidance in assuring proper accounting policies are followed. Consider revising the accounting policies on a regular basis as the church's missions and revenue sources evolve.

Transparency in financial reporting will build trust and understanding on the part of the congregation. Consider asking members of the finance committee to make presentations to the congregation on a recurring basis and be available for questions.

Consider audits of the annual financial statements by either a member of the church or by an independent accountant. Depending upon the financing needs of the church, an audit by an independent accountant might by advantageous, though somewhat expensive.

While tithes and collections are the common source of revenue for churches, the donations are not enough for many churches to maintain their facilities. This is true of declining churches as well as growing churches in low-income communities. Creative funding sources with good partners is key. See the previous chapter for ways to partner with renters and roommates.

Investigate the legal restrictions concerning who can be a partner and what service can be performed on your property. The church is inconspicuous at times, but if discovered, unrelated business revenue can cause expensive problems for a local church.

Conclusion

New and alternative faith communities now form to meet needs in many varied real-life situations.[3] In the real world, other service providers have learned this as well. Ten years ago, the primary way to eat at your favorite restaurant or get carryout was to go to the actual restaurant. Now you can eat their food through a delivery service or perhaps even find their food truck in a neighborhood closer to you.

The stories in this chapter show why the future church must embrace multiple economic models and revenue streams. It will continue to shape our Christian life together.

Strategy Session

With a small group of people, work together through this spreadsheet. Listed to the far-left column of the worksheet are the name of some rooms in your church. Add other rooms in the blank rows. To the right of the room names, fill-in how many hours a week the church uses that space and in the next column fill in how many hours per week outside groups use that space. In the far-right column, calculate the total hours a particular space is used.

---

3. See Tim Shapiro with Kara Fariss, *Divergent Church: The Bright Future of Alternative Faith Communities* (Nashville: Abingdon Press, 2018).

Room in church	Hours per week used by church	Hours per week used by outside group	Total hours used per week	% of use
Sanctuary				
Fellowship Hall				
Offices				
Classrooms				
Courtyard				
Chapel				
Bridal Room				
Parlor				
Gym				

How many hours a week total does your church use its facility?

How many weeks total does an outside group use the facility?

Do outside groups use your facility more than your church?

Are you comfortable with outside groups using your space?

If no outside groups use your space, do you believe they could use your space?

What does the usage data indicate about your ability to open and share your space?

What makes you most anxious about sharing your space?

What risks might be involved in sharing your space?

Share a healthy and an unhealthy story about sharing your church space.

Chapter 6

#MissionLife

Meandering missions are the worst. Sometimes we start out on a mission and proceed in a series of wrong turns and then eventually end in a place we did not anticipate. That destination might be fabulous or it can be horrific. Dr. James Jackson might have felt this way when asked to come down to Miami on a mission to see this new city and discern if he would be their first doctor. Henry Flagler, the man responsible for the railroad in Florida, made the call to Dr. Jackson, who accepted the invitation. Dr. Jackson was living in West Palm Beach, Florida, at the time. The railroad had not yet reached as far south as Miami, so Dr. Jackson had to take his horse to Fort Lauderdale and then catch a boat down to Miami.

Dr. Jackson arrived earlier than expected, so he looked around the city. He found no city, and the sidewalks were made from wooden planks. It was particularly rainy that day, and the wood planks actually moved. Dr. Jackson almost fell into the mud, and the potential fall made it clear to him that he could not be the doctor of this small aspiring "city." He went back to the boat without notifying Mr. Flagler. When he arrived back at the dock, the boat had left. Dr. Jackson learned that the next boat back to Fort Lauderdale would not come for two weeks. He was stuck in Miami. In those fourteen days Mr. Flagler convinced him to stay. Mr. Flagler helped him believe in a city he could not yet see. He became the first doctor in Miami, for whom the major public hospital is named. He also became a charter member of a Methodist church in Miami.

Dr. Jackson believed in something he could not yet see. In some ways he lived by faith. That kind of faith is the future we are experiencing again in our cities, towns, and churches. This kind of faith is like the egg whipped into a really good baking recipe. The egg is the primary ingredient of the special cookie, and without it the cookie would crumble.

A church can have a ten-year plan, but without faith it will be too weak to happen. Faith is the connective tissue of our spiritual life. If not used, it shrinks and is weak, and it cannot move. In physical therapy this is called atrophy.

When I (Ken) suffered a knee injury after I fell off a temporary stage, I spent several days in the hospital and flew home and spent several months with an immobilizer wrapped around my leg. Earlier I reflected on the problem of rigidity, the need to regain flexibility and the importance of muscle memory. There was also an additional challenge.

The sedentary process of healing and recovery also caused the muscles in my leg and around my knee to atrophy, to weaken, almost to the point that I could not even move my knee. I first had to relearn how to take steps by using a walker. I then had to learn how to walk again with crutches. I finally had to learn how to walk again with no assistance. The experience was slow, painful, and successful.

During my time away and through the physical therapy, I considered how much of the accident and recovery reminded me of the church. In so many ways we have become comfortable with where we are, until we have ceased to move. Now that our changing and diversifying culture is affecting our churches with declining numbers, we need to move, and we have forgotten how to do this. Our muscles are weakened and atrophied. Our faith is weakened and atrophied.

We must learn to walk again, even though we are not quite sure where we are going. For the body of Christ to become a movement again, we must engage in the spiritual practices that will help us to become a movement again.

Story

The word *imagination* describes First United Methodist Church of Miami. Imagination filled the original pioneers who developed the city, and the church founders who used their imagination when meeting in houseboats as they sought God's presence in that city. The following narrative contains details that might seem tedious to a leader in a different region or situation. However, the story is told in depth to show how a church is always making choices about how to leverage its property for the sake of the people.

Every forty years or so First Church's holy imagination caused them to dream something new. They first met under a big tent in the financial district, then moved to houseboats, and a few years later inside the walls of old church houses. When divided over abolition of slavery, the Miami Methodists from the north and the south separated into two distinct churches—and eventually Henry Flagler (the railroad executive) gave them both land in what is now downtown Miami. In 1913, White Temple Methodist Episcopal Church moved into its building and two years later Trinity Methodist Episcopal Church, South started worshipping in their new sanctuary. The two buildings were only a few blocks apart. The two congregations worshipped separately for years even after they both came under the same denominational family in 1939.

There were rumors of a merger, but just rumors. This dynamic changed in the early 1960s when White Temple caught on fire early one Sunday morning. The next day the pastor made a big sign in front of the church that read "Burned out but fired up . . . Worship as usual." Perhaps the fire at White Temple, as well as the Methodist leadership in the US civil rights movement, gave the two churches the faith to merge together as one. In 1966, these churches agreed to merge and selected the name First United Methodist Church of Miami. A few years after worshipping in the Trinity Methodist Building, the city of Miami deemed the building condemned. The church would once again use its imagination to lead it to a new home. Like good Methodists everywhere, they formed a committee. The building committee believed that Biscayne Boulevard would be an important part of Miami and they wanted God to be in the center of it! So, they sold property and purchased new property and got into raising funds. Within five years the new church was built and open for worship in 1979.

Holy imagination is not all about property use. Our imagination is always for the sake of the people! First Church started several new churches in the Miami area and even one in China. Mission work around the world was furthered because Miami is an international place, and the gifts of its people gave birth to the first Protestant congregation for Latino people, as well as the Epworth Village Retirement Home. The first Hot Meals program (outside a federally funded program) was started here. Places of civic responsibility occupied many of its members over the years. Some of the social agencies and organization of the city were founded by its members. Over eighty-five ministers and associates have served this congregation.

As one of the most diverse churches in Florida, over twenty-five countries are represented in this church. As people migrated to Miami, they were always welcome at First Church. Immigrants were welcome and folded into the congregation over the first fifty years, and then in the 1970s First Church began working with persons experiencing homelessness in Miami. First Church is a good example of "the Holy Hustle." For more than thirty years it served over 450 breakfasts per week, accommodated 155 showers per week, and each year supplied new shoes and washed the feet of up to 450 experiencing homelessness.

First United Methodist Church of Miami received its first female pastor in 2009. At that time the church was reconciling its annual budget deficit by pulling funds out of the endowment. Cynthia Weems caught on quickly to the pattern and calculated that the church would soon close if continuing to spend in this way. Budgets were cut, which is a tough thing to do in a church. Priorities were refocused to look outward and not simply inward with the church's resources, time, and money. After four years the church was paying its apportionments in full and attained control over its budget and spending. The budget was cut more than once as members would retire and leave Miami or simply relocate to another city for a new job. The tithing revenue of the church was fragile and fluctuated.

Since 2006, First Church supplemented its tithes and offerings with rental income. The renters were many and often changing. The parking lot was the main source of renter income for the church. Miami Dade College was another faithful revenue stream. A church from Burma also rented space on Sunday. Along with these renters were seasonal renters occupying closet space for events and travel. The church learned a new kind of hustle: the real-estate hustle. Ten years into their real-estate rental ventures, life became harder for First Church. Little space was used by the church during the week or even on the weekend. Pastors were spending more time settling renter disagreements than doing marriage counseling for new couples who were moving into the area. The building itself needed renovation and remodeling. The building was also about to approach its forty-year review by the city, which would lead to over half a million dollars in improvements to meet standards. A lot of work was put into five main activities on the campus; a midweek service, a homeless breakfast, Sunday school, a chapel service, and a service in the sanctuary. These five events a week, which totaled about ten hours of use, required many staff and professional levels of bookkeeping and accountability by committees. Many of these processes were required due to one thing: a building. The building not only occupied a large part of the pastors's time but also a large part of the budget. Over 50 percent of the budget every year was expensed to the property, and the church didn't even have a mortgage. In addition, the rental income didn't cover the expenses required of the rental usage.

My (Audrey) first year as the pastor at First Church was a shocking year. I came from a missional church in Florida City. I thought I would be coming to a somewhat traditional and predictable church, but that was not the case. Although the mission at First Church was different, the complexity of the mission was just as daunting and fluid as a missional church that is not yet self-sustaining. The previous pastor did a wonderful job of stopping the financial bleeding and providing stability to the church, but it could not stop the tsunami wave of funerals heading for most downtown churches. During the first year one large "giving unit" passed away and another moved away. I was very quickly feeling the death tsunami. The first year included an HVAC replacement and a water leak in the women's bathroom. By crunching numbers and doing the math it was clear that the church would soon need to make more cuts, but there was nothing more in the budget to cut. The church had some options. It could think about merging with another church or become part of a two-point charge. The church could close and cut its losses before they became painful and dangerous. The church could open the accounts for its endowment for a few years to try and save the church through marketing campaigns and outreach. Or the church could consider something new.

Developers had been circling First Church for a while, and the church had even explored ideas of redevelopment with other pastors, but previously none of the options seemed right at the time. When developers came to the church doors, I could not tell them "Yes, we will sell" and I could not tell them "No, we won't sell." I needed a team. I needed a strategy. The time was right, and the leaders were right, and the faith was present for us to explore the possibilities of redeveloping our property.[1] Our experience was that scripture and strategy were constantly flowing into each other. Thus, in this chapter we hold these two in a greater dialogue.

Scripture and Strategy

Throughout the first two years as pastor at First Church particular strategies and scriptures aided us through a process of change and transformation. We were not perfect in implementing the strategies. There were moments of great trust and high suspicion. There were moments of remembering and times marked by forgetting. Through the process, we learned that the most effective strategy is to trust God and hold onto one another!

Don't Do It Alone—Form a Committee or Team

Strategy

We Methodists are known for committees. Sometimes we call them teams. Younger Methodists say "We don't like committees." Younger Methodists might also say they "love democracy." We need committees to practice democracy. Voices need to be heard, and pastors and leaders need someone to lean on.

1. A change committee needs some of the prior builders of your church. On our committee we included architects for the building that we tore down, so that we could imagine

---

1. For more information about First UMC Miami, visit their website https://firstchurchmiami.org/who-we-are/.

how to redevelop. Their history was crucial, and their excitement about something new was palpable.

2. A change committee needs new people. Believe it or not, people outside your church have opinions about your church and a love for your community. Include them in the conversation, even if you feel they might not have something workable to bring. Our committee included a member of another church who worked in Miami for years. His outside perspective served us well.

3. A change committee needs people who are spiritually mature and can put the purpose of the church ahead of their personal preferences.

Scripture

Methodists encounter sarcasm about forming committees, but we did not invent the method. Jethro, Moses's father-in-law, is to blame. In Exodus 18, Jethro desperately urges Moses to save his health and not to do things alone. He strategizes with him to appoint new judges (the Hebrew means "chieftains"), teach them, and form a counsel for making decisions. Jethro helps Moses form a committee of chieftains.

> When Moses's father-in-law saw all that he was doing for the people, he said, "What's this that you are doing for the people? Why do you sit alone, while all the people are standing around you from morning until evening?"
>
> Moses said to his father-in-law, "Because the people come to me to inquire of God. When a conflict arises between them, they come to me and I judge between the two of them. I also teach them God's regulations and instructions."
>
> Moses's father-in-law said to him, "What you are doing isn't good. You will end up totally wearing yourself out, both you and

these people who are with you. The work is too difficult for you. You can't do it alone." (Exod 18:14-18 CEB)

Throughout our time of change and redevelopment at First Church, I heard Jethro ask me, "Audrey, what are you doing?" I would also ask some of the people, "What are you doing? Stop and don't come to this meeting on your anniversary." In a committee you share the responsibility, you share the risk, and all share in the reward. We are still waiting for that reward. Ironically, after a few years into our committee work, one member said the gift in all the work we were doing so far was getting to know some of the older members of the church in a deeper way. The reward is never the building but always the experience of drawing closer to one another and to Christ.

Adapt an Attitude of Improvisation

Strategy

In the art of improvisation, we continue to be creative and use spread imagination by acting or playing with a process of "yes and. . . . " There is never a period, but always more questions, more imagination, and many possibilities. In creating a new building, we were tempted to go back to build what we already had with the same form and functions. Creativity broke through, however, and resulted in new spaces and interesting ways to use space when we allowed ourselves time to think beyond what we already knew.

Scripture

Since the beginning of God's mighty acts as Lord over creation and history, we have believed that God is going to do something greater than we could imagine. At First Church we celebrated its 120th anniversary while we were just one year into our plans for redevelopment. The theme of our anniversary celebration, "More than we can ask or imagine," was based on Ephesians 3:20-21, in a letter that circulated to many churches.

> Glory to God, who is able to do far beyond all that we could ask or imagine by his power at work within us; glory to him in the church and in Christ Jesus for all generations, forever and always. Amen.

Throughout the process of putting people over property we pray that God would do more than we can imagine.

People Are the Purpose and Priority—Not the Property

Strategy

First Church struggles with this strategy the most, and as their leader I have too. One day an office volunteer came to me and closed the door. She spoke plainly, "Pastor, I have been feeling lately that you are more of a businessperson than a pastor." I went home and cried for hours. I questioned my call and motivations. I confessed to God the times when I put an email message above making a call to a member. I also experienced God's grace and knew that God understood the complexities of my call and vocation in that moment. I prayed God would give me the strength I needed to keep going and would open doors to receive more help in our work. Within six months we were able to hire a full-time operations manager and another pastor to assist in our work.

Scripture

In meeting after meeting, and while gazing at rows of numbers, I was reminded of these words about people:

If I speak in tongues of human beings and of angels but I don't have love, I'm a clanging gong or a clashing cymbal. If I have the gift of prophecy and I know all the mysteries and everything else, and if I have such complete faith that I can move mountains, but I don't have love, I'm nothing. If I give away everything that I have and hand over my own body to feel good about what I've done, but I don't have love, I receive no benefit whatsoever. (1 Cor 13:1-3 CEB)

We could meet a thousand times and build the greatest and most useful church building in the world, but if we don't love our neighbor or one another, we amount to nothing. We will have a great building with few people inside it. Keeping love central has been part of keeping the people as our priority. Our property is simply a tool to help us love more people in the name of Jesus Christ.

"The Church's One Foundation," "Standing on the Promises," and "On Christ the Solid Rock I Stand" are hymns we've sung many times. They allude to the parable Jesus told about the two houses. One house was built on the rock and the other on sand. When the rains came down and the winds came across, the house built on the rock stood strong.[2]

Covenant Love Is Your Way through Conflict

Strategy

Church meetings are occasionally unkind and uncivilized. While working at a camp, I learned the importance of a covenant for outlining how people would treat one another, how people would deal with conflict, and how people would pray for one another.[3] Our covenant carried us through some difficult conflicts. In each redevelopment meeting for First Church we read our covenant. By

2. Matthew 7:24-27.
3. For more information, see https://flippengroup.com.

approaching it in this way, we rarely needed to address a major conflict, since people often behaved well when reminded.

Scripture

In scripture, we are taught that anger is okay, depending on the context and degree. In chapter 3 we mentioned that the only time we see Jesus act out in anger is concerning the proper worship use of temple property. Perhaps the story about Jesus justifies some behaviors when dealing with corruption in the church. Another helpful scripture comes from the Letter to the Ephesians: "Be angry without sinning. Don't let the sun set on your anger. Don't provide an opportunity for the devil" (Eph 4:26-27 CEB). This scripture seems consistent with the mantra "Not today, Satan." Conflict and anger have the ability to completely cripple God's plans for us and our church. Through personal prayer and through external covenants it is possible to address conflict and move forward with a better understanding between the parties involved.

Over-Communicate

Strategy

We all like to be heard. Especially in the church. Sometimes the church is the only place for someone's voice to be heard. By providing multiple tracks for communication to and from a congregation, a change process has a chance. Communication is not limited to talking or gathering into a meeting. Communication can occur in a survey, a poll, and even through a comment box. When conducting a survey or poll, it's important to share the results with the participants. This helps people know you are listening to their needs. Redundant communication about scheduled meetings or when voting is important. Participants in congregations often forget or remember incorrectly. This repetition is heightened for congregations where the membership is aging. One member at First Church suffered with early onset dementia, would often shout out misinformation in meetings. This caused chaos at times, when others would create a narrative around her confusion, which implied that the redevelopment team was not communicating with her. Thankfully, many others in the room correctly remembered information that was given in a prior meeting. Over-communication and documentation are critical when embarking on a big project.

Communication must also be clear to professionals engaged by a church. Church leadership must be clear on what it wants and what it doesn't want. Negotiation will always ensue, so starting at a firm place might not always get you what you want, but it will get you what you need.

Scripture

A particular verse in the Bible encouraged me while preparing a sermon about the sermon addressed to the Hebrews. It is taken out of its original problematic context—for people who stop gathering in worship—but nonetheless these first few words keep us communicating through relationships. "And let us consider each other carefully for the purpose of sparking love and good deeds. Don't stop meeting together with other believers, which some people have gotten into the habit of doing. Instead, encourage each other, especially as you see the day drawing near" (Heb 10:24-25 CEB). This sermon to the Hebrews was presented to an audience more stressed and traumatized by apocalypse than ours, but we also face a temptation to stop meeting. When this happens, when communication stops, a project is in peril as people no longer know what is going on and why it is going on. Sometimes a great way to aid in this is to find fun ways to communicate. Since breaking ground on our new building, we prepared a "Monday Movin' on Update" through a video. The videos focus people on the site, watching the progress, and provide an engaging way to keep communicating.

Through these strategies and scriptures, with the encouragement of the Holy Spirit, First Church made the courageous decision to sell its property. First Church decided to stay downtown and worship on the sacred piece of property that they had purchased years ago. Once again 400 Biscayne Boulevard represents a new future. The church will have 27,000 square feet in the new space (which has forty-nine stories) and will utilize a little over 30 percent of its income from the sale to build out its new space. The church decided to own its space and become a condominium unit through its share in the property. The remaining funds will be in an endowment to produce income interest that will keep the church operating into perpetuity, which is longer than the life of the structure.

The new church building should be complete by March 2022. The church is still meeting in a transitional location, Greater Bethel AME. Greater Bethel is seven-tenths of a mile from 400 Biscayne and has been a gracious host. In deciding where to meet, First Church was surprised that not many buildings—and churches—were supportive of their homeless ministry. The church could have moved temporarily into a high-rise and paid an extreme amount of money each month in rent. Instead, First Church decided to go to Greater Bethel, to partner with a church and help in renovating its spaces and mission in the Overtown area. The partnership has encountered the usual bumps and adjustments, but each partner shares the same mission, which is what makes it work.

Conclusion

John Wesley, founder of the Methodist movement in England, is appreciated for adapting even factories into sanctuaries as a place to preach the gospel. Wesley lived in eighteenth-century England, where the state built and maintained sanctuaries. In his journals, he commended the bishop on the restoration of his residence, which was elegant "though not splendidly." Wesley's letter to the bishop of Armagh also gives acclamation for the "beautifully" restored cathedral and applause for erecting a public library, infirmary, and a free school.[4] It appears that Wesley enjoyed the benefits of the sanctuaries but also understood the balance between beauty and indulgence.

Wesley speaks boldly about Methodist preaching houses, which should be different than sanctuaries or cathedrals. He says,

> Let all preaching-houses be built plain and decent, but not more expensively than is absolutely unavoidable. Otherwise the necessity of raising money will make rich men necessary to us. But if so, we must be dependent upon them, yea, and governed by them. And then farewell to the Methodist discipline, if not doctrine too.[5]

Wesley understood the complexity of property and the priority of people and praise for the community of faith. He wrote, "What is the end of all ecclesiastical order? Is it not to bring souls from the power of Satan to God, and to build them up in his fear and love? Order, then, is so far valuable as it answers these ends: and if it answers them not, it is nothing worth."[6]

Tents, cathedrals, temples, first churches, land, and other assets are tools and resources to aid God's people in the work. None of these assets are morally suspect, and each has revealed God's faithful

---

4. John Wesley, Journal entry (June 22, 1778), in vol. 4 of *The Works of John Wesley*, ed. Thomas Jackson (Grand Rapids, MI: Zondervan Publishing House, reprint of 1872 original), 129.

5. John Wesley, vol. 10, *The Methodist Societies, The Minutes of Conference* in *The Bicentennial Edition of the Works of John Wesley* (Nashville: Abingdon Press, 2011), 931.

6. John Wesley, Letter to John Smith (25 June 1746), vol. 26, *Letters II* (1740-1755) in *The Bicentennial Edition of the Works of John Wesley* (Nashville: Abingdon Press, 1987), 206..

love in worship and in the public square throughout history. When property is valued more than people we miss the love that binds us together and our assets shift from promise to problem. Churches that act in faith to take a property and let God make a promise will be those that see a future.

Whether your church life is a #tentlife, #templelife, #museumlife, #cathedrallife or some type of alternative faith community, the people are its life and the most important part of life is experienced in relationship with God. No particular property is the asset that will save us or the church. Through our #lives and the stories they tell, the strategies they sharpen, and the scriptures they witness to, we can work together toward being faithful and following God more closely.

Strategy Session

Prayer and scripture are essential to any life, especially the life of church that is experiencing change. In what ways can you pray together for your church?

Which strategy and scripture shared in this chapter spoke to you? How might you implement it in a time of change or transition for your church?

What is God stirring in your imagination? Where might God be leading you?

What new discovery did you make about the building your church inhabits?

Chapter 7

#VirtualLife

Story

While writing this book and obtaining feedback, we were often asked if we would address the "virtual church" and the church without a physical building. My (Audrey) response at the time was to limit the scope of the book for churches with buildings, and many of our churches are not in the place to consider virtual church at this point in time.

Nothing breeds innovation more than desperation. As we were finishing up this book, our world and our country plunged into desperate times by a pandemic, and a series of very public racially charged murders. The Church pivoted to worshipping digitally and providing sacred "space" for conversations about race and injustice.

The COVID-19 pandemic moved across our world in the first months of 2020. It became obvious that this virus affects the ways we gather as Christians, which has a profound impact on a shared life together. Andy Crouch and colleagues at Praxis Labs observe that we are not in the middle of a blizzard or even a winter season, but we are entering a "little ice age."[1] The pandemic could have a long-term effect on changes that are already at work in our institutions and churches.

The profound and pervasive way that COVID-19 affected us was stark. It required social (physical) distancing. Public health authorities and governing officials in time saw the necessity of "flattening the curve." The restrictions escalated. No group larger than two hundred and fifty people can meet. No group larger than one hundred can meet. No group larger than fifty can meet. No group larger than ten can meet.

By design, churches are assemblies or congregations. So, we tried to adapt. Some of the response was guided by judicatory leaders. I (Ken) asked that worship happen by live stream, and not in public spaces where we were in one another's presence. In some situations, across the United States church leaders defied the public health authorities. The mandate was publicly debated, and at the same time it resulted in deaths.

Eventually over 95 percent of the population, not including critical infrastructure exceptions, was ordered to stay at home. And so, a reporter from a national newspaper called me and asked the question, "How will you have Easter when the church is closed?"

Of course, this is the question: *When we cannot enter into the building, is the church closed?*

People, Property, and the Lessons of a Crisis

New Forms of Worship

And so, we were called to make the case: The church is not closed! We are simply called to connect with one another in new and

---

1. Andy Crouch, Kurt Keilhacker, and Dave Blanchard, "Leading Beyond the Blizzard: Why Every Organization Is Now a Startup," *Medium*, March 20, 2020, https://journal.praxislabs.org/leading-beyond-the-blizzard-why-every-organization -is-now-a-startup-b7f32fb278ff.

creative ways. This would involve live streaming our worship, and in the weeks and months of the coronavirus, many local churches adapted their oral readings, music, and preaching in this way. In our previous book, *Fresh Expressions: A New Kind of Methodist Church for People Not in Church*, we described the digital world as a "third place," using the terminology of sociologist Ray Oldenburg.[2] Many churches would come to learn that more persons would be accessing their worship services online than their average worship attendance in the pews would reflect. The looming hurdle, of course, is how participants would not merely watch the service but would enter into worship. Yet if we are honest, this is our challenge when we are present in our own sanctuaries.

We discovered in conversations with leaders that many seekers, who were on the edges of the church or who had turned away from religious observance, found it easier to access an online worship service. It felt safe to them. And in the best cases, they experienced grace and hope. One church in its online service included a piece of music by a very gifted young man who had grown up in that church, in Orlando, and had moved to Nashville. In many of our churches we lament the mobility of gifted members and leaders and consider it a loss to the community. In this season, and on that day of worship, there was a profound connection—in a digital world we have more proximity to one another across long distances.

New Contexts for Discipleship

The church is a people, we have recalled, from the song we learned as children. And so, the church exists wherever the story is

---

2.   Ray Oldenburg, *The Great Good Place: Cafés, Coffee Shops, Bookstores, Bars, Hair Salons, and Other Hangouts at the Heart of a Community*, 3rd ed. (New York: Marlowe and Company, 1989).

For extended examples of third places, see Beck, *Field Guide to Methodist Fresh Expressions*, pp. 7–9.

told. For many years we entrusted the church and its leaders to tell the story. By analogy with early Judaism after the loss of the most holy place, the Jerusalem Temple, we are encountering a time when each individual Christian is asked to tell the story at home. Many churches cannot afford a children's director or youth director. Parents are now, once again, asked to teach the stories of faith at home. This trend is even more urgent in the wake of the pandemic. In many ways the pandemic accelerated the slow movement toward church at home.

In an earlier time in ministry, I (Ken) served a large church that often experienced a decline in participation in the summer. As the worship team began to anticipate the next summer, the conversation shifted from assumptions about gathering to how people could be resources where they were. And so, with a focus on the Psalms that summer, a number of initiatives were undertaken—a daily verse went out on Twitter, in the morning and the evening. Across ninety days, the entire Psalter was covered. Individuals were encouraged to have a goal to read through the Psalms in the summer, as a way of deepening their spiritual practice. A poll was taken, and the sermons were drawn from the favorite psalms of the congregation—23, 46, 91, 139. Music was chosen to complement these texts. Two scholars were invited to reflect more deeply on the Psalms.

Gradually, we are adapting to new forms of discipleship. Along with schoolwork at home, parents are also quickly learning how to teach the faith at home. First United Methodist Church in Miami sent Sunday school lessons home to children with a supplemental tele-video call to assist parents in teaching the faith to their children. Parents are learning the classic biblical stories again with their children and participating in deep faith formation with their children. Most teachers would confirm that learning at school is best when it is reinforced at home. In the same way, teaching about our faith is visibly transformative as it is taught and lived out in the home.

In many ways, the pandemic is drawn from our past motivations. In the Methodist tradition we know that Sunday school for children began with a desire to teach children who did not have access to public education. In Sunday school, children would learn their ABCs and 123s. The Bible was taught to children at home.

The Jewish faith has much to teach us in this area. Discipleship happens at the synagogue or Shul, but it is also taught in the home through meals and teachings to children. Fathers and sons and mothers and daughters pray each morning and each evening together. Stories of faith are not reserved for the synagogue but recounted weekly at Shabbat meals. Perhaps this is the great gift of our Jewish friends who have often found themselves displaced and having to adapt their practices and faith in the midst of crisis.

New Ways of Being in Mission

And of course, the church exists wherever we are sent into the world. The coronavirus taught us how attractional we are in our conception of church. The church is a building to which we come; the important metrics are how many gather inside on a Sunday morning. And if we are introspective, we sometimes become competitive about how our metrics appear in relation to a nearby church, or a church of a different tradition. But what happens when attractional church is no longer possible? What happens when a ceiling is placed on how many of us can be together in one place? An extraordinary lesson has been spread through all types of media: we love our neighbor by finding some social or physical distance.

The urgency to discover a new way of expressing ministry practices was spread out of necessity rather than attraction. Many learned to reach out to neighbors and to connect with them. Some of this happened through phone calls, checking in with friends we had been too busy to stay in touch with. Many churches have quickly created phone tree chains. Some of the older members were able to assist in this effort, because they created these trees for years before the pandemic. Some of it happened by honoring the vocations of health care professionals, who would serve on the front lines and bear the cost of a culture that circulated the virus through unnecessary contact. And some of this happened by sharing what we had: our gifts, our tangible goods, our food.

A missional church would also learn from some of our neighbors who often live a precarious existence. One of our pastor friends, Meghan Killingsworth[3] noted that persons struggling with addiction, persons experiencing homelessness, and those in other difficult circumstances experience distance from us, and have much to teach us about how to survive and flourish in a crisis. Mission is always a mutual process of giving and receiving. There are many within our society who have no place to call home and others who live in homes that are unhealthy and possibly dangerous. The pandemic revealed inequities and injustices in access to healthcare. The pandemic became profoundly joined to the justifiable outrage regarding George Floyd, Breonna Taylor, Ahmaud Arbery and Rayshard Brooks. We recognized we were responding to two viruses: a global health crisis and systemic racism. The church's mission is amplified as it works to be a virtual light within the dark places people are finding themselves as they seek physical and spiritual shelter.

Never before has the mission of the church been so clear and sought after. Record numbers of people are attending virtual worship. Significant numbers of people are marching in public spaces to protest racial inequality. Spiritual leaders from monks to priests to pastors are appearing daily on top news networks offering words of hope and practices that ease anxiety. The harvest is plenty in this

---

3. Meghan Killingsworth, "Creative Ways to Connect (with Dan Wunderlich & Meghan Killingsworth)" interview by Bishop Ken Carter, from the *On Mission Together* podcast, March 25, 2020, https://open.spotify.com/episode/1e66GH2epU LrxYerYBVgRn?iontogether=.

season. No doubt after this pandemic passes people will move back to their "Sunday Funday" and busy lives—and faith might be the first thing pushed aside. We are learning during this time of suffering and economic disruption that there is a strong desire in all people for faith, which prompts the great need for the church to be directly engaged with the world. Now, and for some time of social distancing to come, this means engagement with the digital world.

Some churches are reaching completely new people in this time. Some churches are worshipping with three to four times their regular numbers digitally. Some churches are seeing that people come to their virtual church at 11:00 a.m. on Sunday or at 6:00 p.m. on Sunday when they are off work. Virtual worship makes the gospel available to more people in more places in more ways.

Although many futurists anticipated this, we are learning quickly in our own space. We wonder what these new realities and statistics mean for evangelism? Might funds once reserved for home visits and community festivals now be moved to offering online streaming through a church website? Before the pandemic, alternative ways to engage potential new participants would have been very uncomfortable for members. Especially members who did not have internet, social media, or videoconferencing accounts. Now, during, and after the pandemic (though this may be prohibitive for some lower-income households), many homes will have signed up for internet services because they are working from home or because an education must continue for children or grandchildren. More members at First Church have created social media accounts and logged onto our website than ever before! Many are even seeing the benefits of a videoconference call and how it might involve more people because some people do not feel comfortable driving at night or live far away and cannot make it down to the church on a weeknight due to traffic.

While we miss one another and yearn to worship together again, we embrace the benefits of technology for nurturing our faith and for those coming to trust in God. We are pondering what a completely virtual community looks like within a physical church community. As the pandemic crisis fades, people will gradually gather again throughout our society. Some churches are learning that virtual discipleship and worship might be part of our future. Many churches within one church. A physical community and a virtual community. A true mixed ecology of church.

Scripture

Tucked into the story of the woman at the well found in John 4, we find an insight about what constitutes acceptable Christian worship. Jesus says to the woman, "But the time is coming—and is here!—when true worshippers will worship in spirit and truth. The Father looks for those who worship him this way. God is spirit, and it is necessary to worship God in spirit and truth" (John 4:23-24 CEB). Whether at home by the well or in a special sacred space, we are working toward authentic worship, a real connection with Jesus as Lord, which is especially poignant during tough times.

Paul Chilcote comments on authentic virtual worship: "The great adaptation teaches us anew that worship is not about style, worship space, or even direct human contact with others (as significant as this is); rather, it is about encountering God in spirit and truth."[4] Authentic and real worship is laser focused on its goal, which is a connection in spirit and truth with our God. The woman at the well experiences this in her encounter with Jesus. Her encounter was

---

4. Paul Chilcote, "The Great Adaptation," from *The Bishop's Blog*, March 27, 2020, https://www.flumc.org/files/fileslibrary/covid19+related/paul-chiclote-article-2.pdf?fbclid=IwAR2vQf3MEVOvV9oIF7DYfH3C1mQLBCckN77_KFln0WvC_j8JZHoEQXumG24.

honest. She told Jesus some things and asked him some questions, such as "Why do you want a drink from me?" Jesus also surfaced spirit and truth during the encounter, as he told the number of husbands she has had. Jesus spoke to her about the gift of living water and new life. She accepted the new life and worshipped him. The interaction between the woman and Jesus was one of listening, questioning, learning and praising, worshipping in spirit and in truth. Not much else is needed for this worship.

Throughout this book we wrestle with the problem and promise of church land, space, and property. We examined narrative in scripture that points to its necessity and also its futility. When we were required to close the door to our property, to establish social distancing as the best way to avoid harm, many of us feel as though we are in the desert or wilderness. During this time of sheltering in place, like the Israelites with their shrines or rabbinic Judaism with sabbath meals, many of us are experimenting with small altars at home. Our kitchen tables are our offices or homework spaces, and our coffee tables our altars. We are, like the Israelites, called to pitch a tent where we are and deem the space as Holy. We are called to make an altar in our small spaces and worship God in spirit and in truth.

Strategy

Churches are not the only institutions questioning their property and results in a post-pandemic world. Business leaders are living further into the tension of whether provided workspace is needed, whether productivity and innovation can be sustained with all the distractions present in the home. Banks are wondering how much actual space is needed at a local branch. Schools are wondering how much they need to do on campus with unique and differently abled students, and how much learning can happen off-campus.

Individuals are asking if they really need that gym membership or is the home workout routine enough. The whole world is asking what we can cut and live without? The church should not escape this time of introspection and learning. At one end of the spectrum are those who expect churches to boomerang back to the way we used to do things. At the other end of the spectrum are leaders who think that everything must change—a reaction fueled by decades of declining membership and contracting funds. Perhaps your church's wisest strategy moving forward is not a new gym or building or lighting system for auditorium worship. Perhaps your strategic thinking team will choose to shed or repurpose or rent some of your space and fund a more effective digital and virtual platform.

A Mixed Ecology

We might emerge after the pandemic with an unexpected multiplication: a physical church and a virtual church. In a year or two after this book is published, we will yet be learning how to live in this mixed church ecology. In the past, resistance to spending money and time on a virtual community was found among those who benefit from the institutional church and become attached to its buildings and assets. Some leaders forecasted the need for digital engagement with local faith communities over the past two decades. It worked for some very large attractional churches. We don't know yet if virtual worship and digital discipleship are sustainable for *every* faith community in a missional mindset, but with motivated talent and now-inexpensive technologies, some churches are bearing fruit in a crisis. So, we must pay attention to where fruit is growing and adapt our methods to a new way of cultivating and harvesting. We must also consider our behaviors and how those might change over time. Given the toll on health care and unemployment, we are all adapting to new realities concerning people and property.

The challenge remains as to how one truly develops a virtual community. Our institution and trust are built on a "come and see" model. Our theology encourages us to worship a God who is incarnate and who dwelled with us in the flesh. We believe in the body; we are flesh-and-blood people. We enjoy potlucks, and the gift of gab is often a way of practicing our faith as we discern with one another how to live a shared life together with our families. Can this happen in a virtual community? How would a virtual community and a physical community ever meet? Is there a joint mission? Will there be conflicting priorities?

In many ways, the addition of a virtual community keeps all people remembering the main purpose of church—the worship of God and the nurturing of disciples. Few virtual participants will have opinions about what color the parlor should be painted, though they might expect higher production values from our video feed. But few virtual participants want to be on that committee. They can switch channels.

Yet, there still is a need for contact and physical community outside of gathering for the administrative needs of the church. In England, the youth Fresh Expression in Sheffield had over one hundred small groups of teens who had never been to church. One group met at someone's house to bake and talk about life and even faith. Another group met on a basketball court weekly. They played basketball and connected over the issues they had at school and home. All leaders of the group stayed connected virtually. All the different groups came together once or twice a year at a camp where they learned more about faith and got to spend time getting to know one another. This is a potential model for the new mixed ecology challenging the church. Perhaps there will be a resurgence of the Homecoming Service. Possibly this service will be for all who grew up in the church to come home, but also those who are virtual worshippers from near and far to come and be together in the flesh.

If we as a people and a church have learned anything in the season of this pandemic, it is that we are actually not in control. As humans and a human race, we are fragile. As a church both local and institutional, we are fragile. The experience of a pandemic joined to a season of necessary conversation about race and justice teaches us that among our people and in our properties we have much work to do. It is likely that, in a few years, we will see that the pandemic was the beginning of the end for many churches. In a few years, we might also see that the pandemic was the beginning of the beginning for many churches. We are a fragile church and a fragile institution. Our prayer is that the pandemic might motivate us all to take a deep look at who we are as a church and what we have. We pray that this book might assist you in that introspection and that the inner search might lead to spiritual growth and dedicated discipleship. May we listen to what God is calling us to let go. May we listen to what God is calling us to hold close. May we continue to listen, not only to our own story but to the stories of others, the strategies that surround the story and the scripture, which moves us forward in faith. Knowing that when we walk in this way a small piece of heaven is found here on earth—and that is the goal.

HOW WE PRIORITIZE PEOPLE OVER PROPERTY: THINKING ON THE WAY TO ACTION

SEVEN QUESTIONS FOR PASTORS AND KEY LEADERS

1. How can we see our building as a tent in the years to come? (#TentLife)

2. What areas in our sanctuary and building are essential to a deeper trust in God? (#TempleLife)

3. What areas in our property can we let go of or repurpose? (#MuseumLife)

4. How can the church engage the neighborhood and see the world as our parish? (#MrRogersLife)

5. How are we called to think differently about resources and revenue streams? (#RealLife)

6. How has this conversation about property refocused the mission of your church? (#MissionLife)

7. How has the experience of COVID-19 changed our behaviors and led us more fully into the digital world? (#VirtualLife)